FREUD

IN A WEEK

Ruth Snowden

The Teach Yourself series has been trusted around the world
for over 60 years. This academic series of 'In A Week' books
is designed to help people at all levels and around the world
to _____ ___ ____ a key idea in the fields of philosophy,
_____ _____ _____ ember for a lifetime.

Ruth Snowden is a psychology specialist who has written a wide range of books about Freud, Jung and, her particular interest, dreams. Among her books in the Teach Yourself series are *Jung: The Key Ideas and Freud: The Key Ideas*. She also writes children's fiction.

Teach® Yourself

FREUD

Ruth Snowden

www.inaweek.co.uk

IN A WEEK

First published in Great Britain in 2011 by Hodder & Stoughton. An Hachette UK company.

First published in US in 2011 by The McGraw-Hill Companies, Inc.

This revised and expanded edition published 2013

Previously published as *Understanding Freud*

338 Euston Road, London NW1 3BH, by CPI Cox & Wyman, Reading,

The *Teach Yourself* name is a registered trademark of Hachette UK.

British Library Cataloguing in Publication Data: a catalogue record for this title is available from the British Library.

Library of Congress Catalog Card Number: on file.

10 9 8 7 6 5 4 3 2 1

Artworks: Peter Lubach

Typeset by Cenveo® Publisher Services.

Printed in Great Britain by CPI Group (UK) Ltd, Croydon, CR0 4YY.

Hodder & Stoughton policy is to use papers that are natural, renewable and recyclable products and made from wood grown in sustainable forests. The logging and manufacturing processes are expected to conform to the environmental regulations of the country of origin.

Hodder & Stoughton Ltd

338 Euston Road

London NW1 3BH

www.hodder.co.uk

CONTENTS

INTRODUCTION

Sigmund Freud was an Austrian doctor who lived from 1856 to 1939 and he is famous because he founded a new system of psychology that he called 'psychoanalysis'. Psychoanalysis is still the basis of various therapies used today in the treatment of neurosis and psychosis.

Freud totally changed our way of looking at ourselves and our relationships with others. Before Freud, psychologists usually just described and observed behaviour. Freud, wanted to go deeper, to analyse and explain it. His work largely concerns the unconscious, but he did not invent the idea of unconscious mental processes – in fact, the idea had been around for ages. However, Freud was the first to apply the idea to his clinical practice and formulate theories about it. He made people look at themselves more honestly and to try to understand what really goes on under the surface. In many cases this has enabled people to move on from unhelpful or damaging ways of thinking and behaving.

Freud said that we have many inner motives for our behaviour, and that these are mostly sexual. There are also other motives, such as power or aggression. Nowadays Freud is often seen as having claimed that absolutely everything in our minds is sexual. In fact, he realized that not everything could be – otherwise neurotic people would not have to struggle to suppress sexual feelings.

Psychoanalysis has three main aspects: it is a type of therapy, aimed at treating mental and nervous disorders; it also attempts to explain how the human personality develops and how it works; thirdly, it provides theories about how individuals function in society.

Each 'day' we will look at a different major aspect of Freud's life and work – moving from his early ideas about hysteria and the development of psychoanalysis through his major theories about sexuality – most famously the Oedipus complex – and finally to his later investigations into societal phenomena such as war and religion. As you read through this book, however, it is important always to keep in mind that Freud's ideas were not static, but fluid and changing and open-ended. You will see, for example, that his conception of the human psyche underwent quite drastic changes.

This book is only an introduction and what, above all, I hope it will inspire you to do is to go to Freud's own writings. Given the fact that today psychoanalysis has a reputation for being a 'closed shop' and having a penchant for impenetrable jargon, Freud himself wrote in a surprisingly accessible and clear way. His works are available in good English translations. Try, for starters, *The Interpretation of Dreams*. His case studies such as 'Dora', 'Little Hans' and also 'The Wolf Man' also make for fascinating reading. Please explore!

Ruth Snowden

SUNDAY

Freud's life and career

In today's chapter we will learn about Freud's life and career and the influence of his background in the shaping of his ideas. Freud lived and worked in Vienna for most of his life. He was the eldest of eight children and his mother's firm favourite. His parents were ambitious for him and he was a diligent and successful pupil at school. Being a Jew, he had an uneasy relationship with the society in which he lived, which was strongly anti-Semitic. However, Vienna was also a stimulating place to live, both culturally and academically.

Freud trained as a medical doctor, but soon became interested in hypnosis. This led to pioneering work with patients and laid down the foundations of psychoanalysis. He was fascinated by dreams and spent much time analysing his own unconscious. Later on in his career, he formulated theories about how the psyche develops and how societies function. He was a very private person and by his own admission rather neurotic. However, he formed intense friendships. He was a conscientious family man and had six children.

SUNDAY

MONDAY

TUESDAY

WEDNESDAY

THURSDAY

FRIDAY

SATURDAY

FREUD'S EARLY LIFE

Freud was born on 6 May 1856 in Freiberg, Moravia, which was then part of the Austro-Hungarian Empire. The town is now Pr̆íbor in the Czech Republic. In 1860 his family moved to Vienna, where he would live for most of his life. When Freud was born his father, Jakob, was 40 and already a grandfather. Jakob was 20 years older than Amalie, his second wife, Freud's mother. Freud was the eldest of Amalie's eight children and her firm favourite. He later said that this gave him a feeling of invincibility and a great will to succeed.

Young 'Sigi' worked hard at school and his family was very ambitious for him. He soon mastered Greek, Latin, German, Hebrew, French and English and by the age of eight he was reading Shakespeare. Needless to say, he often came top of his class. He had his own room in the crowded home – all the other lesser siblings had to share. He even ate his evening meal apart from the others, and when his sister Anna's piano playing distracted him from his studies his parents had the instrument removed from the apartment.

The family were Jewish by descent, but they did not practise the Jewish religion. Being Jewish was difficult because anti-Semitism was rife in Vienna at the time. Most people in Vienna were Roman Catholics. Two of Sigi's boyhood heroes were the English revolutionary Oliver Cromwell and Hannibal, the Carthaginian leader who fought against the ancient Romans.

Jakob Freud was a wool merchant, but he was not very successful financially. He was married three times and produced many children; as a consequence, he was unable to support Sigmund financially later on. It is important to be aware of Freud's family background and psychological make-up because they influenced his later thinking.

VIENNESE SOCIETY

Freud had a love–hate relationship with Vienna. He was often critical about Viennese people and yet he was very reluctant ever to leave his native city. Several aspects of Viennese society were important in influencing Freud:

- It was a very bourgeois society – middle class, materialistic and conservative.
- It was in a state of economic decline – this led to unemployment, poverty and overcrowding.
- People had a prudish attitude towards sex.
- Men were still thought of as being superior to women. Freud didn't really seem to realize that there was anything wrong with this attitude in his self-analysis.
- The prevailing culture was strongly anti-Semitic. This made it hard for the young Freud when he was struggling to advance his career.
- New movements for social reform were developing, such as early feminism and Social Democracy (a form of Marxism).

A BRIEF OUTLINE OF FREUD'S CAREER

Freud's early ambition had been to study law, but when he entered the University of Vienna in 1873 it was to study medicine. Here he became very interested in zoology and spent a lot of time obsessively cutting up eels. He was greatly influenced by one of his teachers, Ernst Brücke, who was dedicated to the 'mechanistic approach', which emphasized that living things could be understood purely in terms of physics and chemistry. This approach was still unpopular early in Freud's life because it ruled out the possibility of any religious explanations for biology. Freud remained a convinced 'determinist' throughout his life: he believed that all events follow a rigid pattern of cause and effect.

During his clinical training Freud specialized in neurology, finally graduating as a Doctor of Medicine in 1881. He would have liked to have stayed in research, but growing financial pressures and the fact that he wanted to get married meant that he would have to practise as a doctor. He spent the next three years gaining medical experience at the Vienna General Hospital.

In 1885 Freud spent a few months in Paris, studying with a famous neurologist named Jean-Martin Charcot (1825–93). Charcot was experimenting with hypnosis to help cases of hysteria (a nervous disorder with varying symptoms). Freud's experience here was very important because it led him to the idea that the mind could affect physical symptoms. In 1886 he entered private practice as a neuropathologist and began his own work with hysterics. From this work he developed ideas that were to evolve into psychoanalysis. Right from the start, he encountered violent opposition from many other members of the medical establishment because his ideas were so unusual.

Freud's first published book, *On Aphasia*, appeared in 1891. (Aphasia is a neurological disorder in which the patient is either unable to recognize words or to pronounce them.) It soon became clear to Freud that psychological disturbances were indeed at work in many cases of mental illness. This idea was to be the basis of his life's work and one of the main ways in which it differed from that of his contemporaries.

At first Freud concentrated on looking at the causes and treatment of neurosis. Gradually he expanded his theories and became interested in the way the human psyche develops. His work falls into four main phases:

1 **1886–94** During this time Freud studied the causes and treatment of neurosis. At first he concentrated on using hypnosis, but later he developed other forms of therapy that gradually evolved into psychoanalysis.

2 **1894–1901** In this period Freud worked very much alone, doing a lot of self-analysis and developing ideas about the sexual origins of neurosis. At the end of this period he produced two very important books, *The Interpretation of Dreams* and *The Psychopathology of Everyday Life*.

3 **1901–14** Freud began to formulate new theories about the origins of neurosis, which led to a whole system of ideas about how the psyche develops from birth onwards. The psychology that he developed at this stage is often called 'id' psychology. (The id is the part of the psyche that is concerned with inherited, instinctive impulses.)

4 **1914 onwards** World War I made Freud look at people's behaviour in new ways, as he realized that aggression, as well as sexual urges, could be an important factor in behaviour. He began to develop theories about the whole personality and the ways in which people relate to others. This is known as 'ego' psychology. (The ego is the part of the psyche which reacts to external reality.)

Most of Freud's ideas are explained in his book *The Complete Introductory Lectures on Psychoanalysis*. These were originally published in several separate parts, and the ideas were gradually added to and revised.

FREUD'S PRIVATE LIFE AND PERSONALITY

In 1886 Freud married Martha Bernays (1861–1951) and over the years they had six children. The youngest, Anna, became a psychoanalyst. The family went through a great deal of financial struggle and in 1918 Freud lost a lot of money that had been bound up in Austrian state bonds. Martha later insisted that in the 53 years of their marriage they never spoke an angry word. This might be seen as a little suspicious! Freud was rather a private person and he did not reveal many personal details other than in letters to friends.

In academic circles Freud was often seen as being opinionated and rather unconventional, and so much of his work was done in what he called 'splendid isolation'. By his own admission he had a rather neurotic, obsessive personality. He was the kind of person who has to do everything meticulously and accurately and he liked to be in control. His rather obsessive character shows up in various ways. He was very superstitious about certain numbers and he collected quantities of antique statuettes. He was a compulsive smoker and found it impossible to stop, even when he was diagnosed as having oral cancer in 1923. It was not until he had a heart attack in 1930 that he finally gave up smoking.

Freud had a rather neurotic, obsessive personality.

Freud had many close friendships throughout his life, although he was also prone to quarrels and disagreements. Some of his friends developed theories that were thought of as being even more eccentric than Freud's. For example, his friend Wilhelm Fliess was obsessed with the numbers 23 and 28, and thought the nose was an important sexual organ. However, the friendship with Fliess was typical, in that the two men exchanged many ideas and Fliess acted as a useful critic and adviser to Freud.

Among other hobbies, Freud enjoyed playing cards with his friends or going for long walks and looking for mushrooms. People often think of him as a stern patriarch, but in fact his children recalled plenty of happy days when he stopped working and took them for family outings. He did not buy many clothes, and is said to have only ever had three suits, three sets of underwear and three pairs of shoes at a time. However, he was not mean and later in life gave financial support to various friends and students. He enjoyed literature but was not a great music lover, apart from opera.

Following the diagnosis of cancer, Freud suffered many painful medical treatments and surgical operations. He continued to write for the remaining 16 years of his life, publishing mainly philosophical and cultural publications.

In 1938 the Germans occupied Austria, and Freud and his family fled to England. He died in London on 23 September 1939.

SUNDAY

MONDAY

TUESDAY

WEDNESDAY

THURSDAY

FRIDAY

SATURDAY

SUMMARY

Today we have looked at the broad outlines of Freud's life and career and begun to see how aspects of his background may have influenced the development of his ideas. For example, the fact that he was bought up in a Jewish family in what was largely an anti-Semitic culture undoubtedly helped him to stand 'apart from the crowd' and to go against the conventional ideas of his day. Similarly, we have seen how the horrors of trench warfare during World War I propelled him towards new ideas about the role of aggression in the human personality.

Freud's was undoubtedly a complex personality – full of contradictions and paradoxes. He combined clear-sightedness with obsessiveness, generosity with overbearingness, and warmth with steely reserve. This complexity should warn us, as we work through this week, about looking at his ideas in too reductive a way – for example thinking that his theories were all about sex. Freud's thought evolved and changed through a long lifetime and became ever more rich and multi-dimensional.

SUNDAY

MONDAY

TUESDAY

WEDNESDAY

THURSDAY

FRIDAY

SATURDAY

FACT-CHECK (ANSWERS AT THE BACK)

1. In which European city was Freud born?
a) Berlin ❑
b) Vienna ❑
c) Budapest ❑
d) Freiberg, now Příbor ❑

2. Freud's background might best be described as...
a) Working class ❑
b) Aristocratic ❑
c) Middle class ❑
d) None of the above ❑

3. Freud's family was...
a) Roman Catholic ❑
b) Anti-Semitic ❑
c) Jewish ❑
d) Non-religious ❑

4. Freud was a 'determinist'. What does this mean?
a) He was determined to succeed ❑
b) He believed in explaining phenomena by a strict pattern of cause and effect ❑
c) He believed that all phenomena were determined by God ❑
d) He believed that some phenomena were determined by cause and effect ❑

5. In which area did Freud first specialize?
a) Psychology ❑
b) Biology ❑
c) Neurology ❑
d) Nephrology ❑

6. What was the experimental new technique used by the Parisian neurologist Jean-Martin Charcot in the treatment of hysteria?
a) Hydrotherapy ❑
b) Surgery ❑
c) Dream analysis ❑
d) Hypnosis ❑

7. Which are the two main kinds of psychology developed by Freud?
a) Id psychology ❑
b) Sexual psychology ❑
c) Behavioural psychology ❑
d) Ego psychology ❑

8. Which one of the following best describes Freud's personality?
a) Anxious ❑
b) Superstitious ❑
c) Complex ❑
d) Caring ❑

9. Why did Freud move to London?
a) Because he was offered a job there ❑
b) Because he needed specialist medical treatment ❑
c) Because Germany annexed Austria ❑
d) None of the above ❑

10. In which year did Freud die?
a) 1914 ❑
b) 1929 ❑
c) 1938 ❑
d) None of the above ❑

MONDAY

The beginnings of psychoanalysis

Today we will learn about how Freud first developed his revolutionary ideas about the treatment of neurological disorders and the birth of the group of techniques that together became known as 'psychotherapy'.

Freud began his career in medical research. When he began private practice as a doctor, he used hypnosis as a treatment for his neurotic patients. He dismissed another popular treatment, electrotherapy, saying that apparent successes could be explained by the power of suggestion – in other words, he was arguing that mental processes were affecting patients' physical symptoms. This was a radical idea, but Freud was never afraid to go against mainstream thinking. His pioneering work set out to cure neurotic symptoms by releasing suppressed traumatic memories.

At first Freud thought that neurotic symptoms are always caused by traumatic events, but eventually he decided that they could also be caused by repressed sexual urges.

In 1896 Freud went through a period of depression and carried out extensive self-analysis, largely through dream work. He coined the term 'psychoanalysis' in 1896. One of the earliest recorded case histories in psychoanalysis is the analysis of 'Dora', which was published in 1905 in a specialist journal.

FREUD'S MEDICAL TRAINING

Freud entered the University of Vienna in 1873 to study medicine. He did not finish until 1881, so the course took him three years longer than was normal. This was because he really enjoyed research and his interest lay more in this direction than in actually becoming a doctor. He specialized in histology (a branch of anatomy dealing with the structure and function of tissues) as well as neurology. The scientific method he was taught involved systematic observation, measuring and experimentation. This suited Freud's orderly, methodical way of thinking.

SCIENTIFIC RESEARCH

After graduating as a doctor of medicine in 1881, Freud went on to work in the research laboratory at the university. Here he was given an assignment to investigate the sex organs of eels, about which nothing was known at the time. He also studied the nervous system of lampreys (a kind of fish) and his first published article was on this subject. He wrote 20 or so neurology papers between 1887 and 1897.

The mechanistic scientific view insisted that the mind of a human being and an animal such as a frog differed only in their complexity. Even ideas were held to be merely the result of a complicated neurological process. This deterministic view was to remain with Freud throughout his life. He believed that all psychological phenomena, even fantasies and feelings, rigidly followed the principle of cause and effect.

Freud would have happily stayed in medical research, but he realized that he would not have enough money to support a wife and family. He decided that he would have to go into medical practice and spent the next three years gaining practical medical experience at Vienna General Hospital. In 1885 he was appointed as a lecturer in neuropathology at Vienna University. In the same year he wrote an essay about scientific psychology. He was already beginning to embark on his lifelong quest to bridge the gap between the exact science of neurology and psychology, which was still a very poorly understood discipline.

HYSTERIA AND HYPNOSIS

The time that Freud spent working with Jean-Martin Charcot in Paris was to have a profound effect upon his thinking. Charcot was working with cases of paralysis, trying to discover a way of distinguishing between when they were the result of organic disease in the nervous system (i.e. disease relating to particular body structures or functions) and when they were 'hysterical', or neurotic, in origin.

Doctors found hysteria interesting for several reasons:

- The symptoms were very varied. They included memory loss, hallucinations, loss of speech, sleepwalking, paralysis, fits and loss of sensation.
- Only women were supposed to suffer from it. In fact, the word hysteria is derived from a Greek word *hustera*, meaning 'womb'. Charcot disagreed with this and said that men could have hysteria too.
- It baffled doctors because it did not fit in with the anatomy of the nervous system. For example an arm might be paralysed exactly up to the shoulder, even though the nerves do not stop precisely there.

Charcot realized that a patient's own ideas could affect the area of the paralysis. A person's paralysis could stop at a neat line because the person *thought* that the limb began or ended at that line. Charcot discovered that this type of paralysis could be cured, or even induced, by hypnosis. This led Freud to two very important new ideas:

1 To understand hysteria, one needed to look at the patient's psychology, rather than just his or her neurology.
2 Unconscious mental processes can affect behaviour. Although a patient's behaviour could be affected by hypnosis, he or she often did not recall what had happened during the session.

Freud's new ideas may seem rather unstartling to us nowadays, but in the past people had very little understanding of mental illness. Hysterics were persecuted, often locked up or burned as witches, because the unusual and sometimes frightening way they behaved was attributed to the presence of

Hysteria was usually understood as a neurological disorder suffered uniquely by women.

demons. Even Charcot thought that hysterics suffered from a genetic weakness in the brain – for him the cause of hysteria had to be purely physical because he was a strict mechanist. He also thought that only hysterics could be hypnotized. Freud had other ideas and began to think about whether hypnosis could be used as a therapy.

Freud began his own private practice as a neuropathologist in 1886. Two main methods of treatment were then in use with neurotic patients:

● **Electrotherapy** This involved local electrical stimulation of the skin and muscles. Freud considered this method to be useless and said that, when it *did* seem to work, it was only because of the power of suggestion. In other words, he was once again stating that mental processes could affect physical symptoms.

- **Hypnosis** New research was beginning to suggest that this could work on 'normal' people too. So being susceptible to hypnosis might no longer be regarded as a sign of brain damage or genetic weakness.

In 1886 Freud gave a lecture on male hysteria to the Vienna Society of Physicians. He was already being looked upon with scorn because of his interest in Charcot's ideas. This new outrage – the very idea that *men* could suffer from hysteria – met with a fresh wave of hostility. Freud began to realize that his ideas were always going to be unconventional and that he would have to get used to this type of reaction. It was certainly not to be the only occasion when his ideas were to be ridiculed.

NINETEENTH-CENTURY SCIENTIFIC AND MORAL THINKING

It is very important to try to understand Freud's work within the context of the times in which he lived. Prevailing views and ideas included the following:

- The mechanistic view in science, which made it difficult to look at the way in which a person's mind and ideas can affect their behaviour.
- Divisive arguments between scientists and religious thinkers, stemming from the work of Charles Darwin.
- A prudish attitude towards sex, making it difficult to study or discuss anything sexual in a scientific way.
- A patriarchal system, in which men still tended to think they were naturally superior to women.

THE MECHANISTIC VIEW

The normal way of thinking in science in Freud's day followed the rules of positivism. Positivism limits knowledge to things which are directly observable. This goes hand in hand with mechanistic and deterministic approaches. The goal of this way of thinking is simple – you simply describe the facts of what you can experience and observe. Anything else is not science. Positivists try to make general scientific laws about the ways in which phenomena are related. This approach began in the natural sciences and spread into philosophy.

Freud struggled to apply positivism to the way the mind worked. This proved to be tricky, because thoughts, feelings, fantasies and moods are abstract in their nature rather than concrete and are therefore hard to observe. Most psychologists took the positivist stance, but in the developing discipline of psychiatry (the study and treatment of mental illnesses) it was hard to explain these illnesses by means of conventional medicine and mechanistic thinking.

CHARLES DARWIN

Darwin caused great uproar in the nineteenth century with his revolutionary ideas about evolution. Darwin's theory of evolution said that the animals and plants that we see today had all descended from an original simple life form. This process depended on 'natural selection', whereby successful species tended to survive and could therefore hand on their genes. Accidental variations in the genes led to new species gradually evolving, while unsuccessful variations died out.

Darwin's ideas were a direct challenge to the traditional religious view that God had created all the species fully formed from the beginning. Like Darwin, Freud challenged traditional thinking and met with great opposition.

PRUDISH ATTITUDES TO SEX

Sex was almost totally unmentionable in the late nineteenth century. Freud himself said that it was something improper that one ought not to talk about. In such an atmosphere it is hardly surprising that many of Freud's patients had sexual hang-ups.

PATRIARCHY

Some of Freud's ideas seem sexist today, but we have to remember that at this time it was very much the norm for women to defer to men. The man was the undisputed boss

In the late nineteenth century, sex was something that was rarely discussed in public discourse.

within the family and women tended to lead very restricted, boring lives. This, in combination with the strong taboos about sex, meant that women's psychology was as yet very poorly understood.

FREUD'S FIRST IDEAS ABOUT THE UNCONSCIOUS

During the 1890s Freud worked closely with a friend and colleague, Josef Breuer (1842–1925). Breuer told Freud about an interesting case history, the case of 'Anna O.'. Anna was a young woman of 21 who suffered from a bewildering variety of symptoms. She had a nervous cough, speech problems, paralysis of her right arm and neck, and also hallucinations.

Her hallucinations would gradually get worse through the day until in the evening she fell into a strange trance. While in this state, she would mumble odd words.

Anna had recently been nursing her father night and day until his death. This traumatic experience seemed to have triggered her illness. Breuer found that if he repeated her trance words then she would describe her hallucinations to him. This made her a little better for a brief time, but then fresh symptoms seemed to arise. Breuer discovered that when each symptom was traced back to its origin it would then disappear. The origin of each symptom would turn out to be a forgotten traumatic event. While Anna was actually discussing the trauma, her symptoms became very severe.

Breuer also used hypnosis to gain further insights into Anna's problems. His method of curing symptoms by releasing suppressed traumatic memories became known as the 'cathartic method', and the release itself is called 'abreaction'. He stopped treating Anna when she became very dependent on him and fell in love with him. Anna was eventually able to lead a fulfilling life as a social worker and feminist. Her real name was Bertha Pappenheim.

In 1895 Freud and Breuer together published *Studies in Hysteria*. This work presented some rather radical new ideas:

- Negative mental processes can directly affect the physical body and lead to a diseased state. Any traumatic memory that is painful, frightening or shameful in some way can do this.
- These negative memories remain active in the unconscious mind and can alter a person's behaviour. We cannot get rid of them unless they are recalled, i.e. brought back into the conscious mind.
- The banishment of unpleasant memories to the unconscious requires an active process operating at an unconscious level. Freud called this repression process the 'first mechanism of defence', and the idea is one of the cornerstones of psychoanalytic thinking.
- The repressed emotional energy, or 'affect', is converted into hysterical symptoms. These can be permanently erased

by abreaction, when the original trauma is relived and examined in detail.

- A symptom is often 'overdetermined', which means that it is actually caused by several separate events. This makes therapy more difficult.
- Symptoms often prove to be symbolic – for example, a pain in the heart area when a person had a 'broken heart'.

Freud soon found that some of his patients were very resistant to all this unravelling, and he decided that the resistance was sexual in origin. Breuer disagreed with him and there was soon a parting of the ways. Freud slowly abandoned hypnotism and developed a new technique called the 'pressure technique'. The patient relaxed on a couch and the analyst pressed on his or her forehead, announcing that memories would now be recalled. Later on, Freud was to modify this technique again, realizing that it made the analyst too much a figure of authority.

Freud's work was gradually moving towards the idea that there was conflict between two parts of the mind. One part wanted to release a blocked-up emotion but another part found the release unacceptable and refused to acknowledge it. This conflict led to a process that Freud called 'resistance', whereby unconscious ideas are prevented from being released. It was ideas like this that gradually led Freud to his discoveries about the unconscious.

THE REPRESSION OF SEXUAL IDEAS

Freud's theories about psychoanalysis had already begun to evolve during his time working with Breuer. The rift between the two friends came in 1894.

At first, Freud thought that neurotic symptoms were always caused by traumatic events, but case studies eventually led him to the discovery that they can also be caused by repressed sexual urges. He saw the human psyche as constantly striving towards a peaceful state. This meant that any strong emotions, either positive or negative, were seen as unpleasant and therefore needed to be got rid of in order to release tension. This idea was later named the 'Nirvana principle'.

Freud now claimed confidently that *all* neurotic symptoms are caused by sexual experiences, often in early childhood. Sexual satisfaction was therefore the key to happiness and emotional balance. This idea became central to psychoanalytic theory, and Freud remained obstinately adamant about it for a long time. However, we must remember the times in which Freud lived and the prevailing attitude towards sex. Moreover, there was no proper means of birth control. This meant that, once your family was complete, you had to either abstain or, if you were a man, furtively seek satisfaction elsewhere.

THE SEDUCTION THEORY

As a result of early case studies, Freud focused more and more on the influence of sexual experience. He claimed that the key to all neuroses was, in fact, the suppressed memory of an early childhood seduction by an adult. This experience only led to a neurosis if it was suppressed. It then festered in the unconscious, only to re-emerge at puberty as a neurosis.

After a while Freud abandoned this theory, for several reasons. The experience, he noted, was suspiciously common – could it be that some of his patients were inventing the whole thing to fit in with their doctor's theory? Furthermore, some of his own siblings showed neurotic symptoms – surely his own father was not guilty of incest? Freud now had a better idea and argued that some of the 'memories' were in fact fantasies that arose in order to fulfil hidden desires.

This was an important breakthrough – it had dawned on Freud that fantasies could actually be more important than real events in our struggle to understand the human psyche. People had fantasies that were based on instinctive urges. This gradually led Freud to develop his theories about infantile sexuality and dreams. Until then, people had tended to think that children were totally devoid of sexual urges. Once again, Freud was producing new and uncomfortable ideas.

THE PRESSURE TECHNIQUE

Freud seems to have given up using hypnosis completely before he really began to develop his theories of psychoanalysis.

For quite a while after this, he used the **pressure technique**. He would sit behind his patient, who was lying on a couch. When the patient encountered a resistance to talking about something, Freud would apply pressure either to the forehead or to either side of the head. This pressure, he explained, would overcome the resistance. Freud became very keen on this method for a while, and declared that it could unblock resistance in every case. Interestingly, it often gave rise to visual images rather than a fresh flow of words, and frequently patients would recall past scenes that they had previously completely forgotten. These scenes would then unblock a fresh flow of words about what had happened.

Sometimes these scenes, or isolated words that the patient came up with, would lead to fresh insights into the problem he and his patient were working on. But sometimes nothing happened, or the scenes and words that came up would seem to be irrelevant. Usually, Freud would then apply pressure again, and try to get the patient to come up with more images and words. In this way, he helped people to build up chains of related ideas which sometimes did seem to make sense and helped a person to understand what was bothering them.

THE FREE ASSOCIATION TECHNIQUE

Freud gradually began to realize that there was a difficulty with both the hypnosis and the pressure method that he had been using to help his patients. In both cases, the analyst was put in a position of authority and the client was not in control. Using the pressure method also meant that the analyst's voice could interrupt the patient's flow of thought. Even worse, Freud recognized a tendency for the analyst actually to plant ideas that might not have been there to begin with.

Freud therefore developed a modified version of the pressure technique. The patient was encouraged to relax on the couch and to voice whatever thought drifted into his or her mind. The role of the analyst had now changed – ideally he was there simply to guide the patient. In practice, it was not always easy to retain this passive role. This new method was called the 'free association technique'. The idea behind it was that only the patient could really discover the key to the neurosis – this method put the patient back in control of what went on. However, Freud discovered that, as the patient got close to the root cause of the neurosis, resistance was likely to occur.

The patient was encouraged to relax and allow their mind to drift...

From 1894 to 1900 Freud developed many of the theories that we now see as being central to psychoanalysis. He carefully examined and analysed the unconscious mechanisms such as repression and resistance that he saw underlying neurotic symptoms. He also became interested in 'transference' – a word he used to describe the emotional feelings that the client developed towards the analyst. This could involve either positive or negative emotions. For example, the client may actually fall in love with the therapist, as Anna O. did with Breuer. Alternatively, the client might become very hostile towards the analyst.

Freud coined the term 'psychoanalysis' in 1896. The main theories that he was developing during this period were connected with:

● dream analysis
● slips of speech
● infantile sexuality.

FREUD'S SELF-ANALYSIS

In 1896 Freud's father died. For the next three years Freud went through a period of gloom, while he struggled to come to terms with the conflicting feelings thrown up by his father's death. On the one hand he felt love and respect towards his father and on the other he felt hostility and guilt. Freud had a lot of responsibilities by this time. He had six children, and his wife, mother and some of his sisters were all dependent on him. His father's death must have left him feeling very alone in the world. This experience reinforced Freud's belief in the huge importance of the male as the figurehead of the family.

However, his period of darkness (one that we now regard as common when we reach middle age) did have its plus side: it threw him into a period of intensive and intense self-analysis that was to prove very productive. He began to realize that he had long repressed feelings of resentment and rage towards his father and that these feelings were now emerging in the form of feelings of shame and impotence. This revelation led him to examine his childhood memories and his dreams.

Freud realized that unconscious childhood memories often surfaced in adult dreams. For example, he recalled having had sexual feelings towards his mother when he caught sight of her naked when he was a child. The importance of repressed childhood memories, which emerged in dreams and fantasies, became central to psychoanalytic theory.

During his period of self-analysis, Freud wrote *The Interpretation of Dreams*. This book contains analyses of many of Freud's own dreams. He was as objective as possible when working with his own dreams, trying to view himself as he would a client. By the time the book was published in 1900, he was much more confident about his theories and had laid down the main foundations of psychoanalytic thinking. He was using two main approaches with his clients, which are still used today:

● **The free association method** Freud encouraged his patients to make connections between mental images and hidden memories. By talking about these, he found that he could lead the person deeper and deeper into the unconscious.

SUNDAY

MONDAY

TUESDAY

WEDNESDAY

THURSDAY

FRIDAY

SATURDAY

● **Dream analysis** Freud found that dreams were a very
  revealing way of accessing what lay in the unconscious.

A second important book, *The Psychopathology of Everyday Life*,
also appeared at the end of Freud's period of withdrawal, in 1901.
This book deals with what have become known as Freudian slips
of speech and similar mistakes in speech and writing.

THE ANALYSIS OF DORA

Dora was an 18-year-old girl whom Freud saw as a client in
1900. The case is interesting for two reasons. First, it is one of
the earliest recorded case histories in psychoanalysis and one
of the first where dreams were used as the main basis for the
analysis. Secondly, it highlights some possible pitfalls in the
psychoanalytic method. Although the therapy itself was a failure,
the case was used for years as a classic case study for students.

Dora's father had already been to Freud as a patient and he
brought Dora along to Freud in order to 'make her see reason'
(an interesting statement that may give us a clue about the real
source of Dora's neurosis!). She displayed typical hysterical
symptoms, such as fainting, depression and losing her voice. By
the time she came to see Freud she had also threatened suicide.

The story is a complicated one, but the main point was that
Dora had a crush on Frau K., who was her father's mistress.
Meanwhile Frau K.'s husband, Herr K., had allegedly made
sexual advances to Dora since she was 14. A tangled web
indeed. Dora vehemently and consistently announced that
she hated Herr K., but Freud interpreted this as meaning that
the root of the problem was that she was secretly in love with
him. The more Dora declared her hatred, the more Freud
announced that this was clear evidence of repression of her
true feelings. Heads I win, tails you lose.

Eventually, after 11 weeks in therapy, Dora quit. She had
been labelled by now as a lesbian, and the analysis certainly
did nothing to alter her sexual orientation. However, Freud
claimed that she had eventually accepted the idea that she was
in love with Herr K. This perhaps illustrates how pigheaded and
persuasive Freud could be, once he got the bit between his teeth!

SUMMARY

Today we have focused on how Freud developed his initial ideas about the connections between neurological symptoms displayed by patients and the inner workings of their mind – that is, their psychology. While such ideas may seem commonplace to us today, in the nineteenth century they flew in the face of 'positivist' science, which concerned itself solely with the observable and the measurable. Freud dared to take science into uncharted territory.

Resistance to Freud's ideas was compounded by the fact that he insisted on the central role played by sex in the production of neurological disorders – at a time when sexuality was deemed to be a private, 'unmentionable' concern. Moreover, he seemed intent on exploring the sexual impulses and experiences of women and children. For the overwhelmingly male establishment, this seemed a step too far. Nonetheless, Freud did find a clientele for the therapeutic treatments that he based on his radical ideas and theories.

SUNDAY

MONDAY

TUESDAY

WEDNESDAY

THURSDAY

FRIDAY

SATURDAY

FACT-CHECK (ANSWERS AT THE BACK)

SUNDAY

MONDAY

TUESDAY

WEDNESDAY

THURSDAY

FRIDAY

SATURDAY

1. How might we best describe the science of Freud's time?
a) Overly influenced by religion ❑
b) Concerned only with observable phenomena ❑
c) Open-minded ❑
d) Metaphysical ❑

2. Which of the following were once thought to be characteristics of 'hysteria'?
a) Suffered only by women ❑
b) Suffered only by children ❑
c) A wide variety of symptoms ❑
d) Often seemed to contradict the anatomy of the nervous system ❑

3. What was the therapeutic method developed by Freud's colleague Josef Breuer?
a) Exploring a patient's dreams ❑
b) Releasing a patient's memories of a traumatic event ❑
c) Getting a patient to talk about their childhood ❑
d) None of the above ❑

4. What was the famous case in which Breuer and Freud put forward their ideas?
a) 'Little Hans' ❑
b) 'Dora' ❑
c) 'Anna O.' ❑
d) 'Greta Z.' ❑

5. Freud parted ways with Breuer because...
a) Breuer thought that Freud was stealing his ideas ❑
b) Freud insisted that the repressed traumatic events were *always* sexual ❑
c) Freud insisted that both men and women suffered from hysteria ❑
d) They simply no longer got on ❑

6. Freud gave up the 'pressure technique' because...
a) It caused his patients physical discomfort ❑
b) It gave too much authority to the analyst ❑
c) The patent did not have enough control ❑
d) There was a risk of the analyst planting ideas in the patient's mind ❑

7. Freud replaced the 'pressure technique' with...
a) Free thought ❑
b) Free analysis ❑
c) Free speech ❑
d) Free association ❑

8. What event in 1896 prompted Freud's depression and period of self-analysis?
a) The death of his father ❑
b) The death of Josef Breuer ❑
c) The discovery that he was suffering from cancer ❑
d) The repeated rejection of his ideas by the establishment ❑

9. Which of the following are key ideas that emerged from Freud's self-analysis at this time?

a) The importance of fantasies ❑
b) The importance of dreams ❑
c) The importance of sexual memories from childhood ❑
d) All of the above ❑

10. Which of the following best describes the significance of the case of 'Dora'?

a) An early successful example of Freud's psychoanalysis ❑
b) One of the earliest recorded examples of Freud's psychoanalysis ❑
c) An example showing the possible pitfalls of Freud's psychoanalysis ❑
d) None of the above ❑

SUNDAY

MONDAY

TUESDAY

WEDNESDAY

THURSDAY

FRIDAY

SATURDAY

TUESDAY

Freud, dreams and the unconscious

Freud believed that it was during sleep that the conscious mind releases its hold and that dreams represent a kind of bubbling up of the unconscious. A therapist cannot force a person to understand what is going on in their unconscious. Only dream analysis and free association can really begin to unravel the symbolism involved in neurotic symptoms.

According to Freud, dream symbols often disguise childhood sexual issues, which are thus prevented from entering the conscious mind and waking the dreamer. He also stressed that all dreams are wish fulfilments. By exploring the hidden desire symbolized in a dream, one can therefore begin to unravel a neurosis.

Freud also gradually extended his psychoanalytic studies to explore the 'normal' human mind, looking at jokes and 'Freudian slips' as well as dreams. He soon discovered that the unconscious plays a huge part in determining the behaviour of ordinary people. This step was important because psychoanalysis was no longer limited to abnormal psychology, and Freud's ideas became accessible to a wide audience.

DREAMS AS WISH FULFILMENT

People have always tended to see some of their dreams as wish-fulfilment fantasies. We use phrases like 'in your dreams' or 'not even in my wildest dreams'. Freud claimed that dreams were *always* driven by the need to fulfil a wish. In its simplest form, a dream directly expresses a wish. For example, Freud describes the dream of a young mother who was cut off from society for weeks while she nursed a child through an infectious illness. In her dream she met lots of well-known authors and had fascinating conversations with them. Again, when Freud's little girl Anna was sick and not allowed any food, she dreamed of strawberries, omelette and pudding. This type of direct wish-fulfilment dream is common in small children.

Freud saw dreaming largely as a form of regression to childhood and the instinctual forces and images that dominate this time of our lives. He believed that recent events and desires played a minor role in dreams. In this respect, Freud's ideas differ from modern theories about dreams, where recent and current events are regarded as very important. Freud argued that the wishes represented in dreams must be infantile desires. He admitted that this was not invariably the case, but he insisted that it was usually true, even when the infantile desire is not at first suspected.

In cases where it seemed impossible to unravel a hidden wish fulfilment, Freud cunningly used two possible explanations:

1 The patient is in a state of negative transference to the analyst and is deliberately producing awkward dreams in order to trip him or her up. To back this up, Freud cites a case where a barrister friend dreamed that he had lost all his cases. Freud and he had been rivals at school and Freud had always beaten him. Therefore he is identifying with Freud in the dream and hoping that *he* will lose. This means that the dream conceals a hidden wish fulfilment.
2 The patient is employing mental masochism and the dream is satisfying a masochistic urge, which is in itself a form of wish fulfilment.

These explanations could perhaps be seen as further examples of Freud's own stubbornness when he wanted to prove a theory!

During and after World War I Freud had experience with shock and trauma victims who relived recent ghastly wartime experiences in their dreams. This led Freud to question his earlier insistence that dreams were always wish fulfilment and always harked back to childhood.

The world of dreams could lead the analyst deep into the unconscious.

DREAM MECHANISMS

While it might be obvious that the simple type of dream can be a wish-fulfilment fantasy, can the same be said of a nightmare or an anxiety dream? Freud explained this by saying that each dream has both a manifest content (which is consciously remembered) and a latent content (which is not recalled until

SUNDAY

MONDAY

TUESDAY

WEDNESDAY

THURSDAY

FRIDAY

SATURDAY

analysis). If the dream is properly interpreted, one will still find a hidden wish fulfilment lurking beneath the apparent meaning of the dream. The latent content of the dream is actually the cause of the dream. Freud proposed that two mechanisms were at work here:

1 The sleeping mind begins to create a dream, based on a wish fulfilment.
2 The mind is shocked by the wish and imposes censorship on it. This causes distortion in the way the wish is allowed to appear in the dream.

Freud gives an example of this process. A patient of his dreamed that she wanted to hold a supper party, but various things kept going wrong. There was not enough food; it was Sunday, so she couldn't order more to be delivered; the phone was out of order ... and so on. Analysis of the dream revealed a hidden jealously of the friend whom she had been going to invite to the supper party. She was afraid that her husband was attracted to her friend, but fortunately the friend was skinny, and as her husband preferred plump women she felt reasonably safe. However, she was damned if she wanted to fatten her up with a special supper party!

Freud said that the latent content of the dream could be revealed only through dream analysis and free association. The latent aspect of the dream is seen as being the important part because it contains the real meaning, which has been censored. The thought processes of the unconscious brain are irrational and incomplete. The goal is simply to evade the censor and allow the dream ideas to be expressed somehow. Freud suggested that there were various mechanisms at work, which allowed the dream wish to be expressed, but in a distorted form:

● **Displacement** Feelings about a situation are not expressed directly, but are associated in the dream with something different. The manifest content of the dream is very different from the latent content, but the feelings themselves remain very much the same.
● **Condensation** Two or more ideas are fused together in the dream. In this way, a dream image may have more than

one root cause. Much deeper meanings may lie behind the dream image.

- **Symbolization** Dream images or ideas are often symbolic, so that they secretly represent other things. According to Freud, most dream symbolism is sexual in nature.
- **Resistance** Freud said that we tend to forget dreams because of dream censorship, which still tries to prevent the dream ideas from entering conscious thought.

METHODS OF DREAM INTERPRETATION

Freud maintained that every dream, even the most seemingly trivial, has a meaning. He realized that this was not a new idea – even the Greek philosopher Aristotle (384–322 BCE) saw dreams not as sent by the gods but as the mental activity of the sleeper. The prevailing mechanistic view of Freud's time tended to view dreams as being the meaningless result of physical processes in the sleeping body. Freud disagreed, pointing out that dreams have been viewed throughout history as being full of hidden meaning. Freud described two ways in which dreams were usually interpreted:

1 **The symbolic method** For example, in Joseph's dream in the Bible, seven fat cattle are followed by seven thin ones that eat them up. This was interpreted symbolically as showing the seven years of famine that would follow seven years of plenty. This method tends to fall down where dreams are very confused and unintelligible.
2 **The decoding method** Here, a fixed key (such as those found in many dream books today) was used to interpret the meaning of the dream. Freud said that this was not scientific because the original key could be wrong.

Freud discovered that while his patients were relaxing and free associating ideas, they began to tell him about their dreams. He saw their dreams as further symptoms, and the method he used to unravel them was really the same free-association method he used for other problems. During the process of free association and dream analysis the patient had to be relaxed and feel safe. This meant that two things could happen:

1 The patient and analyst could both pay closer attention to what was going on in the patient's thought processes.
2 They were able to remove the critical censor that normally sifts thought processes as they arise.

In effect, Freud's new method was reversing the critical, repressive attitude that prevailed in Vienna at the time. He was encouraging people to look at themselves in an uncritical way. Freud helped people to analyse each bit of a dream separately, even though this was often a painstaking process.

Freud gave advice about dream interpretation that is still very helpful today:

● To interpret a dream is hard work and requires perseverance.
● After working on a dream, one should leave it alone – fresh insights may come later.
● Dreams often occur in groups, with a common underlying theme. An insight into one dream may unravel a whole series of dreams.
● Something that seems trivial or superficial in a dream may actually be masking a deep insight.
● It is important for the analyst to pay attention to all the client's remarks, however trivial they may seem on the surface.

FREUDIAN SYMBOLS

Freud believed that much of a dream's content was disguised by means of symbols. Freudian symbols within dreams have become one of the best-known aspects of psychoanalytic thinking. Freud believed that symbols frequently have more than one meaning and that correct interpretation can only be arrived at by analysing the dream. To understand symbols, he used a combination of two methods:

1 an exploration of the dreamer's own associations
2 using the analyst's knowledge of common dream symbols to fill in the gaps.

Freud's own ideas about what dream symbols mean are notoriously sexual. For example, he suggested the following interpretations:

- Sticks, knives, umbrellas, and other pointy objects represent the penis.
- Boxes, chests, ovens, cupboards and other containers represent the uterus.
- Movement up and down ladders, stairs, seesaws, etc. represents having sex.
- Playing with a little child represents masturbation.

Freud developed a highly sexualized version of the traditional dreamer's dictionary...

However, Freud warned that it was not always easy or straightforward to find the correct interpretation of a dream symbol.

ORIGINS OF DREAMS

Freud noticed that a good deal of dream content came from recent events or emotional reactions. He explained that often these were actually distortions, masking deeper emotional issues that were connected to the recent events by long trains of association. In the same way, he maintained that childhood memories were also linked to recent events by association. Thus the dream is often not really about current affairs at all.

THE DIVISIONS OF THE MIND

Initially, Freud decided that there were two states of consciousness or parts of the psyche:

1 **The conscious mind** This is the part of the mind that is aware of its thoughts and actions. It is where all conscious thought processes occur, and is the source of ideas and understanding. It is concerned with logical thinking, reality and civilized behaviour.

2 **The unconscious** This is the part of the mind that is repressed, the place where we put anything that our conditioning does not allow us to look at. Information in the unconscious cannot easily be accessed. Much of our past history lies here too, some of which can be recalled only under hypnosis.

Eventually, Freud concluded that this simple division was not completely accurate. He therefore proposed the existence of a third level:

3 **The preconscious** This is where information is stored that is not conscious at the moment, but can easily be recalled when needed. Imagine the psyche as a house. The conscious mind is the living quarters, while the preconscious is a filing cabinet where information is stored ready for reference. The unconscious is the cellar, or perhaps a loft, for which you need a ladder to enter.

THE THEORY OF THE UNCONSCIOUS

Freud saw the unconscious as being the part of the mind that lies outside the boundaries of consciousness. It was constructed by repression of ideas that were too painful or dangerous to be allowed to remain in the conscious mind, and also by sublimation – the rechannelling of instinctive drives for which an acceptable outlet cannot be found. These two processes were governed by laws of transformation. Freud saw the primary content of the unconscious as being sexual in nature, formed from sexual desires and urges that have been repressed.

Primitive instinctive urges had to be repressed and pushed down into the unconscious in order for human society to function properly; otherwise everyone would just act on impulse all the time and there could be no rules or structure. Each child had to go through a series of developmental stages where this repression of instincts was gradually accomplished – for example, they had to be potty trained, learn not to hit other children and so on.

Freud believed that the sex drive in particular was so strong that it constantly threatened to force its way up to the surface and take over, but he did not think it was the only drive that governs human behaviour. In his later writing he suggested that there were a huge number of instincts, or drives, in the psyche, which can all be grouped into two main categories: Eros (the life instinct) and Thanatos (the death instinct). Urges linked to Thanatos were destructive and therefore worked against the sex drive, which is obviously basically creative in its nature.

Freud realized that not everything in the unconscious is repressed material: some of it is just stuff that happens not be conscious at the moment. This is why he initially decided that there had to be a third area – the preconscious – containing information that we are not thinking about at a given moment, but which is easily accessible when we need it. An example of this could be a foreign language that we were taught at school but have not really used since.

Later on, Freud thought up a more complex model of the mind, based on these early ideas, where he suggests that the mind is composed of three parts – the id, the ego and the superego. This model will be discussed later in the book.

THE PLEASURE PRINCIPLE AND THE REALITY PRINCIPLE

Freud suggested two opposing processes that control normal human behaviour:

1 **The pleasure principle** This pushes people towards immediate gratification of their wishes. It is the tendency behind all natural impulses and basic urges. It is linked to the unconscious and it is impulsive, primitive and disorganized. According to Freud, it governs us from birth and basically concerns the gratification of our sexual urges – Freud did not seem to consider other basic drives such as hunger when he was talking about this drive. The pleasure principle is always the main motive force of the unconscious.

2 **The reality principle** As a person matures and has to operate in a social environment, the opposing force, the reality principle, comes into play. This involves conscious, logical thinking, and it allows us to delay gratification in order to get on with everyday life.

Freud used the word 'libido' to describe the sexual drive, which he claimed was the driving force for most behaviour. The reality principle causes libidinal energy (i.e. sexual energy) to be redirected into safer or more socially acceptable behaviour. This unconscious redirection is called 'sublimation'.

According to Freud, psychic conflicts arise as a result of the conflict between sexual drive (ruled by the pleasure principle) and survival (ruled by the reality principle). After a while, however, he changed his mind about the two forces being in opposition. He decided that they actually worked together because both led to a decrease in tension. This decrease in tension, he believed, was the purpose of all behaviour.

It seems typical of Freud's pessimistic outlook on life that the 'pleasure principle' is actually all about avoiding tension and pain! It is not about pleasures such as love, joy, fun and friendship. Freud always tended to view any powerful emotion as negative, something that needed to be expelled in order for a person to feel comfortable. According to Freud, a person's character is determined by the way he or she has channelled libido into more acceptable activity. If libido is blocked up without an outlet, then neuroses or other psychological problems develop. Psychoanalysis is all about finding out what urges have been blocked up, and why.

After a while, Freud discovered a problem with the idea of the pleasure principle. He found that patients who suffered from neuroses caused by trauma tended to keep on endlessly acting out the original scene in their imagination. Small children also do this in a more concrete way, by repeatedly acting out nasty experiences. This probably gives them some sense of control over the original incident. Freud eventually began to evolve a new theory about a 'death instinct' as an attempt to deal with this problem.

PARAPRAXIS

'Parapraxis' (the plural is 'parapraxes') is a term often used for the now famous 'Freudian slip'. Freud became interested in parapraxes because they occurred frequently in the lives of perfectly 'normal' people, and seemed to him to demonstrate that the unconscious was at work. His popular book *The Psychopathology of Everyday Life* is all about parapraxes. The title of the book is interesting in itself because the word 'psychopathology' (meaning the study of abnormal mental processes) implies that Freud believed parapraxes to be symptoms of abnormality or disorder, despite their universal occurrence.

Freud identified a whole list of different forms of parapraxis, such as:

- forgetting peoples's names
- forgetting something one intended to do
- slips of the tongue or pen

- misreading or mishearing
- losing or temporarily mislaying things
- bungled actions and accidents
- remembering things wrongly.

Freud claimed that none of these are actually innocent, accidental mistakes. They all reveal the unconscious at work on a cover-up job again, rather like the dreaming process. Thoughts that are painful or socially unacceptable are disguised by means of a Freudian slip. The slip is seen, not as a silly chance mistake, but as a subconscious mental act.

The Freudian slip... Even accidents could be interpreted as examples of parapraxis, Freud believed.

Slips of speech are often caused by the influence of something that is connected to the misspoken word by a chain of thought. Sometimes they occur when the person anticipates a taboo word coming up, or perhaps feels that the conversation is getting uncomfortably close to revealing his or her true feelings. In fact, any kind of parapraxis arises as a result of two different intentions in a person's mind that are acting in opposition. They reveal what the person is *really* thinking.

According to Freud, all parapraxes occur in this way and if they are analysed this will nearly always prove to be the case. However, it is not possible actually to prove that his theory is true. Other psychologists argued that parapraxes are caused by factors such as fatigue, excitement or distraction. Freud admitted that this was true, but insisted that such an explanation missed the point – such conditions simply make it easier or more likely for slips to occur.

FORGETTING PROPER NAMES

Freud gives an example where, try as he might, he could not recall a place name. In the end he had to ask his wife and daughter for help. They were amused, saying that of course he would forget a name like that – the place was called Nervi. Freud had quite enough to do with nerves in his daily work, and so pushed the name out of his mind. Very often, a wrong proper name will intrude in place of the correct one. When this occurs, the two are usually connected by a train of associations. The subconscious wants to forget the correct name because it has painful or embarrassing associations. Or it may just be connected with a topic one has had enough of, such as work, as in the example given by Freud.

FORGETTING CHILDHOOD MEMORIES

Many childhood memories are not consciously recalled by the adult. Freud observed that children frequently remembered trivial events rather than important ones. He says that both these facts indicate a process of displacement going on – the child substitutes a trivial memory in order to conceal a painful one. Freud calls this type of memory a 'concealing memory', and says that they form a large part of our total memory bank. He seems to overlook the possibility that sometimes children might seem to remember trivia because for them those are actually the things that have assumed importance.

ACCIDENTS

Even accidents, such as tripping over, are parapraxes. Freud says that they show unconscious feelings being expressed in a physical way. We all know examples of people who seem to

SUNDAY

MONDAY

TUESDAY

WEDNESDAY

THURSDAY

FRIDAY

SATURDAY

get themselves injured almost on purpose in order to be able to lap up attention. Conversely, we sometimes 'accidentally' hurt another person when we feel hostile towards them, or we may break an object such as a hideous vase because of a subconscious desire to get rid of it.

Freud gives various examples of 'bungled actions'. For example, Freud forbade one of his patients to contact a girl with whom he was madly in love. All the same, the patient accidentally used her telephone number instead when he was trying to contact Freud. This shows that bungled actions, like other errors, are often used to fulfil wishes that a person is consciously trying to deny.

SLIPS OF THE TONGUE

These are very common and one can easily observe amusing ones in everyday conversation; for example: 'He entrusted his money to a savings crank.' This category also includes Spoonerisms, where bits of words are swapped around; for example: 'The student had tasted the whole worm.' The slip of the tongue can often be seen to be transparently covering up what the person would really like to have said.

FORGETTING FOREIGN WORDS

Freud said that we are less likely to forget a word completely in our native language – a slip is more likely to appear instead. He goes on at great length about an occasion when he was trying to remember the name of an artist called Signorelli. He kept getting Botticelli or Boltraffio in his mind instead. His explanation for this covers about six pages in *The Psychopathology of Everyday Life* and involves a complicated diagram with such labels as 'death and sexuality' and 'repressed thoughts'. It is all very interesting and ingenious, but somehow the process seems rather unlikely. Is the unconscious really that desperate to conceal fairly trivial thoughts? And how does it work out such a complex series of connections so quickly? The problem with this type of analysis is that it relies mainly on the free-association process. This method usually leads quite rapidly to the uncovering of supposedly 'significant material', even if you start with an innocent, neutral word.

SLIPS OF THE PEN

These, like slips of the tongue, are common and easily recorded. Freud tells of an incident when he came home from holiday in September, but wrote the date as 'October 20th'. The explanation was that he was experiencing a lull in his work after the holiday period and had a client booked in to see him on the October date. So the slip was a kind of wish-fulfilment process, of wishing that the date would hurry up and arrive.

JOKES AND THE UNCONSCIOUS

Freud was also interested in the way jokes demonstrate the workings of the unconscious. His book *Jokes and Their Relation to the Unconscious* appeared in 1905. In it is quite a collection of jokes, mainly Jewish ones (unfortunately, many of the jokes do not translate very well). The main point he makes was that some of the mechanisms used in jokes are the same as those used in dreams. For example, one word is substituted for another, or condensation is used. He claimed once again that repression and sublimation of unconscious material is taking place.

Freud identified two categories of jokes:

1 **Tendentious jokes** This type is dependent on indirect expression of hostility or sexual urges. The category would include the classic mother-in-law joke and the dirty joke.
2 **Innocent jokes** These depend on verbal ingenuity. The category would include puns and riddles.

The first category is the one in which Freud was chiefly interested. They allow the joker to get around internal inhibition by expressing an urge indirectly. For example, schoolboy humour often involves rude jokes which are told to relieve adolescent tension. The urge being indirectly expressed may be either sexual or aggressive. Freud eventually claimed that *all* jokes are in fact tendentious, the innocent ones being a kind of foreplay, leading up to the tendentious ones!

All Freud's work on dreams, the pleasure and reality principles and parapraxes is actually looking at ways in which the ego *defends* itself. If the ego finds an idea too painful, embarrassing or socially unacceptable, the idea is repressed. The unconscious then finds endless little ways of letting the ideas leak back out.

SUMMARY

Today we have focused on Freud's evolving ideas about the unconscious and how certain human phenomena such as dreams, slips of the tongue and even jokes can offer glimpses into its murkiest recesses and our normally hidden urges and desires. For Freud, dreams in particular were a key link between the unconscious and conscious mind – he famously called them the 'royal road to the unconscious'.

As we have seen, Freud's exploration of phenomena such as dreams and jokes began to take psychoanalysis away from the confines of abnormal psychology and towards an understanding of human psychology more generally. He began to develop 'models' of the human psyche and argued that there were psychic drives, principles and mechanisms that were common to all human beings, whatever the state of their mental wellbeing.

Freud's understanding of the unconscious still largely shapes the way most of us think of human psychology today, even if many of his ideas have been adjusted, challenged, or even dismantled by the 'experts'.

SUNDAY
MONDAY
TUESDAY
WEDNESDAY
THURSDAY
FRIDAY
SATURDAY

FACT-CHECK (ANSWERS AT THE BACK)

1. What is the title of Freud's 1900 ground-breaking publication about dreams?
   a) *The Analysis of Dreams* ❏
   b) *The Interpretation of Dreams* ❏
   c) *The Royal Road to the Unconscious* ❏
   d) None of the above ❏

2. Which of the following statements does *not* describe Freud's understanding of dreams?
   a) Dreams can offer insights into the unconscious ❏
   b) Dreams are all about wish fulfilment ❏
   c) Dreams occur when the conscious mind is at its most unguarded ❏
   d) Each night's dreams merely replay our conscious concerns from the previous day ❏

3. What kind of content does the analyst seek to uncover during dream analysis?
   a) Manifest ❏
   b) Sexual ❏
   c) Traumatic ❏
   d) Latent ❏

4. Which of the following is *not* a mechanism of dream distortion?
   a) Condensation ❏
   b) Disassociation ❏
   c) Symbolization ❏
   d) Resistance ❏

5. Which of the following describe(s) Freud's approach to dream analysis?
   a) Literal ❏
   b) Collaborative ❏
   c) Symbolic ❏
   d) Attentive ❏

6. What is the preconscious, according to Freud?
   a) The hidden, repressed part of the psyche ❏
   b) A stage in early childhood before we are fully aware ❏
   c) An accessible but temporarily stored-away part of the psyche ❏
   d) None of the above ❏

7. What name did Freud give to the two main drives that operate in the unconscious?
   a) Eros and Anteros ❏
   b) Eros and Thanatos ❏
   c) Eros and Hypnos ❏
   d) Eros and Phobos ❏

8. The reality principle enables us...
   a) To see our situation as clearly as possible ❏
   b) To fulfil our desires as quickly as possible ❏
   c) To delay gratification of our drives so that we can get along with day-to-day life ❏
   d) All of the above ❏

9. For what is the libido another name?

a) The unconscious ☐
b) The life instinct ☐
c) The death instinct ☐
d) The sexual drive ☐

10. Which of the following is *not* a possible example of parapraxis?

a) Crashing a friend's car ☐
b) Having an argument ☐
c) Forgetting someone's name ☐
d) Losing your house keys ☐

SUNDAY

MONDAY

TUESDAY

WEDNESDAY

THURSDAY

FRIDAY

SATURDAY

WEDNESDAY

Freud's
theories
about sex and
sexuality

Today we will look at the central role played by sex and sexuality in Freud's ideas and his understanding of what these words encompassed. Theories about sexual development became important in psychoanalysis from an early stage and Freud extended the concept of what was considered to be 'sexual'. He did this in order to support his theory that neuroses were caused by sexual problems and that neurotic symptoms therefore had sexual meaning.

Freud studied what he saw as being sexual deviations and drew the conclusion that the sexual instinct is a lot more complex than people had previously assumed, and that it has to struggle against various mental resistances. He decided that the sexuality of neurotics has usually remained in, or been brought back to, an infantile state.

The popular view in Freud's day was that sexuality lay dormant until puberty. Freud challenged this view, saying that sexual impulses are present from birth, but are soon overcome by a progressive process of repression. Childhood and puberty are fraught with sexual pitfalls which can lead to any number of problems in later life.

FREUD ATTACKS CURRENT THINKING

Freud published his book *Three Essays on Sexuality* in 1905. In it he explained that it was difficult to define exactly what was meant by the word 'sexual'. To say that it meant everything to do with the differences between the two sexes was too vague. On the other hand, the view that it was only concerned with actual genital contact between two people of the opposite sex was too limiting. Furthermore, to say that it meant everything to do with reproduction would leave out obviously sexual things such as kissing and masturbation. Freud concluded that the word 'sexual' concerned *all* these things and more.

The acceptable view of sex during Freud's time was that it involved bringing the genitals into contact with those of somebody of the opposite sex, and that this naturally entailed kissing, looking at and touching the other person. This behaviour was concerned only with reproduction, and did not surface until puberty when the body became sexually mature. Freud caused uproar when he suggested that people needed to take a much broader view in order to study sex scientifically. He pointed out the following:

- Homosexual people are often attracted sexually only to members of their own sex. They may even find the opposite sex repellent. Freud called this group of people 'inverts'. For them, sexuality has nothing to do with the reproductive process.
- For other people, the sexual drive disregards the genitals or their normal use. They may be excited by inappropriate body parts, inanimate objects, and so on. Freud said that the words 'sexual' and 'genital' therefore had very different meanings. Freud calls this group of people 'perverts'.
- Psychoanalytical research had shown that neurotic problems and perversions were often caused by early childhood sexual experiences. As children were not supposed to have a sex life, this suggestion caused a particular furore.

What Freud was really doing was to extend the concept of what was 'sexual'. He did this in order to support his theory that neuroses were caused by sexual problems and that neurotic symptoms therefore had sexual meaning. He found that neurotics often showed great resistance to any mention of sex. Their sexual urges were often very strongly repressed. Normal people, on the other hand, satisfied their sexual urges in ordinary sexual activity and in dreams.

SEXUAL DEVIATIONS

Freud defines various types of sexual deviation, which he divides into two groups:

1 deviations in respect of the 'sexual object', i.e. the person, or thing, from which the sexual attraction comes
2 deviations in respect of the 'sexual aim', i.e. the sexual act that a person is driven towards.

This division seems rather artificial and even Freud seems to get muddled about it, saying, for example, that fetishism could go into either category.

INVERSION

This is the word Freud uses for homosexuality. He recognizes different types of behaviour in this category:

● Some people are attracted exclusively to their own sex.
● Some are attracted to both sexes.
● Some people turn to their own sex when the need arises, e.g. in prison.

Freud goes on to say that some inverts accept their sexuality as a natural state of affairs, whereas others are horrified by it and see it as a pathological compulsion. In the more extreme cases the person has been an invert from a very early age and is more likely to have accepted the state of affairs.

Freud was not able to identify one single sexual aim among inverts. Nor was it possible to find a satisfactory explanation for the origin of inversion. But he did say that it points us to one important fact – that the sexual instinct does not always draw us to the same object. In fact, it is surprisingly common for deviations to occur.

ORAL AND ANAL SEX

Oral and anal sex were considered as perversions by Freud. He said that a feeling of disgust prevents most people from indulging in either perversion. This is one of the natural repressive mechanisms that make people develop in the direction of 'normal' sexuality. However, the repression can be so forceful that the genitals of the opposite sex seem totally disgusting too. Freud found this to be a common reaction among hysterics.

FETISHISM

Fetishism occurs when the normal sexual object becomes replaced by an object that bears some relation to it. The fetish object is usually non-sexual. For example, it might be a different part of the body such as the hair or the feet; or it could be an inanimate object such as an item of clothing. Freud said that fetishism usually occurred as the result of a sexual experience in early childhood, and a symbolic train of thought later connects the fetish to the sexual urge.

TOUCHING AND LOOKING

Freud regarded tactile and visual stimulation between sexual partners as perfectly normal. They constituted a perversion only if:

- they were restricted only to the genitals
- they were involved with the overcoming of disgust – for example in voyeurism, or in people who enjoy watching excretory functions
- they totally supplanted the normal sexual aim.

SADISM AND MASOCHISM

Sadism means the desire to inflict pain on the sexual object. Masochism is the desire to receive pain from the sexual object. Freud said that the roots of these two perversions are easy to detect. In the normal male, sexuality has a strong element of aggression – there is the desire to overcome resistance and dominate the sexual partner. In sadism this urge gets out of hand. (He does not seem to explain how this would account for sadism in women.) Masochism seemed rather further removed from the normal sexual aim. Freud said that it was probably caused primarily through guilt and fear. He saw it as a kind of extension of sadism, turned in upon the self. He added that there was definitely a connection between cruelty and the sexual instinct, but he was not able to explain why.

Freud drew several conclusions from his study of sexual deviations:

- The sexual instinct has to struggle against various mental resistances. This is probably a mechanism to keep the sexual instinct restrained within the range of what is considered to be 'normal'.
- Some perversions are complex in their origin. This shows that the sexual instinct is a lot more complicated than people had previously maintained.
- The sexuality of neurotics has usually remained in, or been brought back to, an infantile state.

This discovery brought Freud to the study of infantile sexuality.

INFANTILE SEXUALITY

The popular view in Freud's day was that sexuality lay dormant until puberty. Psychologists writing about child development generally omitted any reference to sexuality. It was improper to mention sex much at all, so to imply that children thought about it was the ultimate horror. Once again, Freud stuck his neck out. He suggested two main reasons for the silence about infant sexuality:

1 Sex was a taboo subject.
2 Most people tend to forget what happens to them in early life until they reach the age of six to eight years.

Freud thought that this second aspect was strange because small children show plenty of evidence of awareness and insight. However, early recollections could be brought to light under hypnosis. Freud therefore proposed that there was a special process of 'infantile amnesia' that went into action to repress thoughts about sexual experiences.

He claimed that sexual impulses are present from birth, but are soon overcome by a progressive process of repression. This process comes about as the child discovers that it has to comply with various rules in order to fit into society. Feelings of disgust and shame begin to arise and these suppress the sexual urge. The process of infantile amnesia is the forerunner of, and basis for, the process of hysterical amnesia in adult life.

According to Freud, infantile sexuality is concerned not only with the genital region. It shows up at different stages of development in various parts of the body, such as the oral zone, the anal zone and finally the genital zone. The aim of all infantile sexual activity is to get satisfaction by stimulating an 'erotogenic zone'. (This is an area of the body where certain stimuli, especially rubbing, produce feelings of pleasure.) After a while, at about age six to eight, this early sexual activity goes dormant until puberty. This is known as the 'latency period'.

INFANT EXPLORATION OF SEXUALITY

Children are naturally curious about sex. Freud says that they explore sexuality in various ways – for example, they want to know where babies come from. Many of them are dissatisfied by nursery explanations such as the stork fetching them. Misunderstandings are common too – for example, children may think the baby is born through the anus because they are used to the idea of faeces appearing in this way.

Children are also curious to find out about the opposite sex. There was not so much scope for this in Freud's day because children were kept 'decently' covered up. The eventual revelation was often very traumatic according to Freud. For boys it led to what Freud termed a 'castration complex', in which, having observed that the little girl had no penis, the boy was terrified that he would somehow lose his own. For girls it led to a terrible 'penis envy', in which the little girl was overcome with jealousy at the male organ and started wanting to be a boy.

Freud also claimed that if children witnessed adults having sex, they invariably thought that they were fighting. Glimpses of menstrual blood on sheets or underwear only served to confirm this horrid suspicion.

THE STRUGGLES OF PUBERTY

According to Freud, the sexual focus goes through various different stages during childhood. Sexual changes in the physical body begin to occur at puberty and change the whole pattern of infantile sexuality.

- The child's first sexual feelings arise from sucking at the mother's breast. At this very early stage the mother is the sexual object.
- Next comes the stage of infantile sexuality where the child is excited by the sensations in its own body. This stage is 'autoerotic' – the infant derives pleasure from its own body, so the child's own body is the sexual object.
- At puberty the child begins to be attracted to members of the opposite sex. A new sexual object now has to be discovered.
- At this point the two sexes diverge because different functions emerge for their sexual aims. According to Freud, the development of inhibitions of sexuality appears earlier in little girls. Obscurely, he views the early autoerotic and masturbatory activity of the infant as being 'wholly masculine' in both sexes. He explains that in little girls the erotogenic zone is the clitoris, which is homologous (fundamentally similar in structure and development) to the tip of the penis.
- At puberty the sexual organs grow and get into working order. This causes new sexual tensions. Freud says that in boys there is a great increase in libido, and this is fairly straightforward. But the unfortunate girls are attacked by a fresh wave of suppression because they have to overcome their previous masculine sexuality and transfer the erotogenic zone from the clitoris to the vagina. This process is very difficult and is a frequent cause of neurosis, especially hysteria.

Freud's theories of female sexuality and development now seem highly dubious and misinformed. However, it is important to remember that he developed these theories a century or more ago, when female sexuality was very poorly understood. Astoundingly, the true structure and function of the clitoris has only been very recently revealed.

SUNDAY

MONDAY

TUESDAY

WEDNESDAY

THURSDAY

FRIDAY

SATURDAY

According to Freud, childhood and puberty are fraught with sexual pitfalls and one false step along the way can lead to any number of problems in later life:

- The object choice begins with the child's early relationships with parents and carers. It is only later diverted away to other people by incest taboos.
- The child can get stuck at any stage in the sexual development process. This is called 'fixation'.
- Repression of sexual urges may lead to psychoneurotic illness, such as perversions.
- Very often the libido finds an outlet in another, non-sexual field. This is called 'sublimation'.

Freud suggests that neurotic people may have a greater tendency to be affected by early sexual experiences, and to become fixated. He saw one of the main causes of fixation to be the early seduction of the child by another child or an adult. He suggested that sexual deviations could arise through a combination of several causes, such as:

- a compliant constitution and/or precocity
- increased susceptibility to early sexual experiences
- chance stimulation of the sexual instinct by external influences.

SUMMARY

We have seen today how extraordinarily daring Freud's exploration of sexuality was, given the puritanical attitudes that still held sway in the early twentieth century – in public discourse at least. We should remember, however, that some of his contemporaries were also engaged in a parallel project – we have only to think, for example, of the erotic paintings of the Viennese artist Gustav Klimt or the plays and stories of Arthur Schnitzler. Perhaps most courageous of all was Freud's extension of his researches into areas previously hidden – female and infantile sexuality, for example.

We have also seen, nonetheless, how Freud's ideas were shaped, not to say limited, by the prejudices and intolerances of his times. His ideas about women's sexuality and homosexuality have quite rightly been much criticized. In this respect, Freud's ideas – because of the very reach of their influence – can be argued to have played a negative, even oppressive, role in the lives of women and sexual minorities through the twentieth century.

SUNDAY

MONDAY

TUESDAY

WEDNESDAY

THURSDAY

FRIDAY

SATURDAY

FACT-CHECK (ANSWERS AT THE BACK)

1. Which one of the following best describes Freud's understanding of sexuality?
a) Restricted ❑
b) Broad ❑
c) Tolerant ❑
d) Permissive ❑

2. Which sexual behaviours did Freud describe as 'inverted'?
a) Fetishes ❑
b) Oral ❑
c) Anal ❑
d) Homosexual ❑

3. To what cause did Freud ascribe perversions?
a) Childhood sexual experiences ❑
b) A conscious rejection of appropriate sexual behaviour ❑
c) A failure to control one's sexual urges ❑
d) Out-of-control sexual fantasies ❑

4. Which of the following did Freud *not* consider to be an example of sexual deviance?
a) Oral sex ❑
b) Anal sex ❑
c) Kissing ❑
d) Sadism ❑

5. Why, according to Freud, had infantile sexuality remained unacknowledged?
a) People believed that childhood was a time of innocence ❑
b) Discussion of sex, in general, was taboo ❑
c) People repressed their memories of childhood sexual experiences ❑
d) All of the above ❑

6. What, according to Freud, could cause children to experience sexual trauma?
a) The sight of the genitalia of the opposite sex ❑
b) The sight of adults having sex ❑
c) The sight of their own genitals ❑
d) The sight of their mother's breasts ❑

7. At what point does the child first experience sexual pleasure?
a) In the womb ❑
b) During birth ❑
c) During breastfeeding ❑
d) During puberty ❑

8. What is 'fixation'?
a) Any obsession ❑
b) Falling hopelessly in love with someone ❑
c) Where an individual becomes stuck at a certain stage during his or her childhood psychosexual development ❑
d) None of the above ❑

9. What is sublimation?
a) The channelling of the sex drive into a non-sexual pursuit ❑
b) Taking pleasure in awe-inspiring landscapes ❑
c) The repression of the sex drive ❑
d) Excessive attention to the libido ❑

10. Which one of the following
    descriptions do you think
    best characterizes Freud's
    understanding of female
    sexuality?

a) Tentative ❏
b) Blinkered ❏
c) Ground-breaking ❏
d) Courageous ❏

SUNDAY

MONDAY

TUESDAY

WEDNESDAY

THURSDAY

FRIDAY

SATURDAY

THURSDAY

Freud's theories of psychosexual development

Freud gradually developed his ideas about childhood sexuality in order to try to explain how people developed into social beings. Eventually, he divided psychosexual development into several defined stages. Each stage followed on from the one before in a biologically determined manner and the way a person coped with each stage influenced their adult personality. Freud did not explain these stages all at once in a neat and logical order, but added to his theories over a period of many years.

Freud was very much concerned with the ways in which the libido can become blocked or redirected, taking the form of neuroses in the adult personality. In order to explain the mechanisms involved in this process, he eventually developed a new tripartite model of the psyche, made up of the id, ego and superego. These parts of the psyche can readily come into conflict, creating anxiety and neurosis when they are not held in balance.

THE ORAL STAGE

This is the first stage of psychosexual development and it lasts from birth to about one year old. The infant indulges in sucking various parts of its body, especially the thumb, an activity that follows on from sucking the mother's breast. The sucking is rhythmic, and often involves rubbing movements as well. Freud says that these later lead on to masturbation. The activity is very absorbing and comforting and often sends the infant off to sleep.

Sucking is obviously by far the most important activity at this stage in the baby's life, and so the mother becomes the first love object. The baby feels love or hate accordingly, as the breast is offered or withdrawn. The source of love is also the food source, and it gradually becomes a source of sexual pleasure. Freud broadened the concept of sexual pleasure, allowing it also to encompass sensual pleasure.

Withdrawal of the breast is seen as withdrawal of love and fixation at this stage is called 'oral fixation'. Freud says that this fixation sometimes occurs when babies have not been breast-fed. It manifests later on in all sorts of ways, for example:

- thumb sucking in older children
- chewing gum, pens, pencils, fingernails, etc.
- smoking, excessive eating or drinking
- feeling a constant need to be loved.

This seems to cover the vast majority of the adult population, so presumably none of us is very good at getting past this first stage!

THE ANAL STAGE

This lasts from about the age of one to three years old, and coincides with the 'potty training' phase, when the child learns to control the bladder and bowels. The child feels very proud when he or she produces stools and often sees them as part of him- or herself. However, the adults who care for the child may express disgust, especially if the child produces offerings at an inappropriate time or place. The child has to learn when the activity is socially acceptable and when it is not.

The child soon finds that it can gain power over the adult by withholding stools, or by producing them at the wrong time. According to Freud, producing or withholding stools is all very pleasurable. When potty training begins, the baby often deliberately hangs on to its stools. This is because it wants to enjoy the erotic pleasure of producing the stool in private! Producing a huge stool also apparently stimulates the mucous membrane of the anus. (A more acceptable argument today is that stool retention can happen because the baby is constipated and producing huge compacted stools hurts.)

The anal phase is where social conditioning really begins to come into play. The child is praised for being 'clean' and getting things 'right'. On the other hand, repressive guilt and disgust begin to appear when the child gets it 'wrong'. Fixation at this stage can take more than one form:

● 'Anal expulsiveness' follows on from producing stools inappropriately. Adults stuck at this stage are often scruffy, disordered and anti-social.

The anal retentive...?

- 'Anal retentiveness' follows on from withholding stools. The adult stuck at this stage is compulsively neat and tidy, orderly and conformist.

Parental disapproval at this stage can also lead to a later neurotic obsession with dirt and cleaning.

THE PHALLIC STAGE

This stage is from about three to five years. The genitals now become the erogenous zone and the child starts to masturbate. The infant genital zone is stimulated frequently by washing, rubbing dry, peeing and so on. The child soon learns to stimulate the area itself, by rubbing with the hand or by pressing the thighs together. Freud's views on this stage reveal a misogynistic attitude – the phallus is seen as all-important, and in fact he seems to regard it as the *only* sexual organ. This is the stage where sexual differences are often discovered by children, giving rise to the castration complex in boys and penis envy in girls. Freud says that girls see themselves as already castrated and never really recover from the shock of the revelation about penises.

This is also the stage when the notorious 'Oedipus complex' emerges. (A complex is a related group of ideas that are usually repressed and can cause emotional problems and conflicts.)

THE OEDIPUS COMPLEX

Freud formed his ideas about the Oedipus complex during the period of his own self-analysis. In a letter to Fliess at this time, he describes discovering that as a small boy he had been in love with his mother and jealous of his father. The Oedipus complex is named after a character in an ancient Greek story. Oedipus was the son of King Laius and Queen Jocasta of Thebes. It was prophesied that Oedipus would murder his father and marry his mother, and so, in fear of this, his father had him left to die on a mountain soon after his birth. However, the baby was rescued by shepherds and brought up by a foreign king and queen.

Eventually, Oedipus met his father by chance on the road to Thebes and murdered him in a fit of rage. He then went to Thebes and rid the city of a tiresome Sphinx, which had been eating anybody who was unable to answer her riddle correctly. Oedipus answered the riddle and was rewarded by being made king, and so ended up unknowingly marrying his mother, Queen Jocasta. When Oedipus found out what he had done, he blinded himself as a punishment.

In putting forward his theories on the Oedipus complex, Freud argued the following:

- All little boys of about four or five fall in love with their mothers.
- The boy expresses his desire in various ways, such as by announcing that he is going to marry her, or by insisting on climbing into bed with her all the time.
- He becomes curious about her naked body.
- The boy wants total possession of the mother and becomes jealous of his father; he wants to kill him to get him out of the way.
- Because the father is obviously so big and powerful, the boy is afraid that he will be punished by his father castrating him. This fear eventually makes him abandon his mother as a sexual object.

The picture Freud paints for girls is even more bizarre and he is typically much less clear about his views.

- The little girl is also involved with lusting after the mother initially, but then comes the awful revelation that she has no penis.
- The little girl believes she has lost hers and (for some obscure reason) blames her mother for this.
- The little girl cannot fear castration because she sees herself as already castrated. For her, the corresponding fear is a fear of loss of love.
- She then turns to the father as a sex object, hoping that he will impregnate her. The resulting baby would partly make up for the lost penis.
- The conflict is gradually resolved as she turns her attention away from her father towards other men.

Freud saw the Oedipal conflict as being basic to psychosexual development. Failure to resolve the incestuous conflict results in neurosis later in life.

To us today the theory can seem contrived, but this is partly because it has been overstated by Freud and he seems to make the mistake of generalizing on the basis of his own childhood experiences. However, if we look at the theory again we can see some elements of truth in it:

- Small boys do sometimes fall in love with their mothers, and may consequently get very jealous of the father.
- The same can be true with small girls and their fathers.
- The blinding of Oedipus is symbolic of the shock, self-disgust and self-punishment that may arise when dark, inner wishes are revealed. Many people do feel guilty about their own natural sexual urges.
- Men and boys sometimes do fear damage to the penis – it is rather vulnerable, after all. In the past, little boys were actually threatened with having their penis cut off if they masturbated, which would obviously lead to considerable anxiety.
- In Freud's day, girls were seen as being very inferior and making a baby was probably one of the few important things they felt they could do.

THE LATENCY STAGE

According to Freud, the feelings from the Oedipal stage are eventually suppressed and the sexual drive goes dormant until puberty. In fact, subsequent research has shown that this is not really the case. On the contrary, sexual curiosity, sexual play and masturbation all gradually increase. However, in Freud's time such activity would largely have been concealed from adults.

THE GENITAL STAGE

The final stage in development is the genital stage, which takes place from puberty onwards. There is now a renewal of sexual interest and a new object is found for the sex drive. This is seen as the final stage, the completion of development, which

For Freud, successful psychosexual development led to 'normal' sexual interest in the opposite sex.

seems rather odd considering the angst and confusion most of us go through in our teens and early adulthood! The Oedipus complex is now resolved and the natural aim of the sex drive becomes sexual intercourse with an opposite-sex adult.

Freud insisted that psychosexual development was central to all social and emotional development. His theories about the way the child's sexuality developed provided a model of the way the whole personality developed. But Freud did not say that the whole mind was concerned only with sex – otherwise there would be no conflicts. A lot of the opposition to his theories has arisen because of the way he defined what was 'sexual'. For him, the concept had a much broader meaning than just sex itself. Nevertheless, most people now feel that his emphasis on the sexual was exaggerated.

ID, EGO AND SUPEREGO

In 1923 Freud proposed a new dynamic model of the mind. (A dynamic model in psychology is a simplified description of a system, emphasizing motives and drives.) Freud's new model involved three main parts: the id, ego and superego. These are not physical parts of the brain but represent different aspects of the way we think. They are an attempt to explain the apparent battle that goes on between different levels of consciousness. Conflicts between them result in anxiety and stress. Anxiety acts as an alarm signal that something is wrong; the commonest cause of anxiety, according to Freud, is sexual frustration. A particular source of anxiety is attached to each developmental stage.

THE ID

From the Latin word for 'it', the id is the primitive, unconscious part of the mind that we are born with. It is a dark, inaccessible area, seething with instinctive urges, and its only reality is its own selfish needs. It is the source of the motive force behind the pleasure principle. As a child develops through the various oral, anal and phallic stages, it begins to realize that the world 'out there' is real too. This new awareness is closely linked to sexual development. Gradually, the child begins to realize that it cannot always instantly have what it wants, and begins to suppress the id urges in order to fit in with society. Adults who are selfish or impulsive may be unable or unwilling to suppress the id. The desires of the id are commonly expressed in dreams.

THE EGO

From the Latin word for 'I', the ego is the part of the mind which reacts to external reality and which a person thinks of as the 'self'. The ego is where consciousness comes from, although not all of its functions are carried out consciously:

● The ego tells us what is 'real'. It is a 'synthesizer' or a 'maker of sense'.

- It is practical and rational, and is involved in decision making.
- Anxiety arises from the ego. This is seen as a mechanism for warning us that there is a weakness somewhere in the ego's defences.
- A whole system of unconscious defence mechanisms protects the ego.
- The ego is seen as being rather weak in comparison with the id, but it is better organized and more logical, so that it usually maintains a tenuous upper hand.

Freud explains, somewhat confusingly, that the ego is part of the id, which develops in order to cope with threats from the outside world. He compares the ego and the id with a rider and his horse. The horse supplies the motor energy, but the rider decides where to go. The ego constantly has to devise little plans to satisfy the id in a controlled way. For example, a child is hungry but knows that it will have to wait until teatime until it gets a slice of cake.

THE SUPEREGO

The superego...

This is the part of the mind that acts like an 'inner parent', giving us a conscience and responding to social rules. A very small child is amoral and has little sense of inhibition. Any controls over its behaviour are provided by the parents and carers who look after it. In normal development this state of affairs slowly changes. The superego develops as the Oedipus complex begins to be resolved. As the repression of Oedipal urges commences, the child feels a mixture of love, fear and hostility towards the parents. Gradually, a sort of inner parent evolves and the child has feelings of guilt and of being 'watched' and controlled. This is the superego:

- The superego gives us our sense of right and wrong, pride and guilt.
- It often gets us to act in ways that are acceptable to society, rather than to us as individuals. For example, it might make a person feel guilty for having extramarital sex. The superego incorporates the teachings of the past and of tradition.
- It monitors behaviour, decides what is acceptable and controls taboo urges.
- It is bossy, always demanding perfection of the ego.

The way the superego works is, in a sense, opposite to that of the id. The id wants to satisfy the needs of the individual, regardless of what society wants. Like the ego, large parts of the superego can operate in unconscious ways. Freud acknowledges that the distinctions between id, ego and superego are not easy to grasp and that the three are not always sharply separated. If an adult has achieved a reasonably mature, mentally healthy personality, the id, ego and superego will be acting in a balanced way.

ANXIETY

Conflicts between the different aspects of the personality result in anxiety and stress. Freud said that anxiety acts as an alarm signal that something is wrong. He identified three types of anxiety:

1 **Realistic anxiety** This arises from real events in the external world, perceived by the ego.
2 **Neurotic anxiety** This arises from the id, and often seems enigmatic and unfocused. It is not necessarily connected with external events in the real world.
3 **Moral anxiety** This arises from the superego – it is the voice of the conscience, telling us when something is 'improper'.

Anxiety from all three sources feels similar, and in fact anxiety can arise from a mixture of different sources at the same time. Anxiety is closely associated with feelings of guilt. It can also present itself in the form of phobias and hysteria. Hysterical anxiety can come as a very severe attack, which does not necessarily have an obvious source in the external world.

Anxiety...

SUNDAY

MONDAY

TUESDAY

WEDNESDAY

THURSDAY

FRIDAY

SATURDAY

Freud says that the most common cause of anxiety is sexual frustration. This begins in infancy, when the mother is not present, or when the infant sees an unfamiliar face. (Remember that Freud sees the mother as the sex object at this stage.) A particular source of anxiety is attached to each developmental stage. For example, at the phallic stage it is the fear of castration that causes anxiety and at the latency stage it is a developing fear of the superego. As the ego gets stronger and more clearly defined, the anxieties weaken, but traces of them usually remain. Neurotics remain infantile in their attitude to danger and consequently suffer a great deal from anxiety.

DEFENCE MECHANISMS

Defence mechanisms arise in order to protect the ego from too much anxiety. Without them, anxiety can become a threat to mental health. Defence mechanisms are used unconsciously and, within reason, they are healthy. However, they can easily become too forceful and damaging, requiring much mental effort to sustain them, and masking issues that really need to be addressed. In this case they become merely a strategy for hiding from anxiety.

REPRESSION

This is one of the most common defence mechanisms and it forms the basis for many of Freud's theories. Undesirable information is stored away in the unconscious, so repression is really a form of forgetting. We may repress something so that we do not have to deal with painful feelings and memories. People can lose whole blocks of time in this way after a traumatic event and conscious efforts to recall events may have no effect. This can apply both to emotional traumas and traumas caused by external events such as war.

DENIAL

Denial is closely related to repression, but this time the person refuses to accept the *reality* of a situation. This is sometimes acceptable as a short-term defence, but becomes dangerous if the situation never gets properly dealt with. For example a person finds a suspicious lump somewhere on their body and, fearing it might be cancer, may forget all about it rather than go to the doctor.

DISPLACEMENT

This is another common defence mechanism that arises as a result of repression. Because a person cannot release a basic feeling such as anger, it builds up and is then directed towards another person, animal or object that has nothing to do with the original situation. For example, if a person has a bad day at work, rather than confront the boss they may come home and vent their frustration on the family.

PROJECTION

This is almost a combination of denial and displacement. It is once again a result of repression, whereby a person is unable to recognize the reality of his or her own behaviour. The result is that taboo urges or faults are projected outwards on to another person. For example, the bossiest member of the household covers this up by accusing one of the others of being bossy.

FANTASY

Most people indulge in a certain amount of fantasy and daydreaming in order to make life more bearable. This is perfectly normal and can actually be quite positive – for example, dreaming of that holiday in Spain might motivate you to work a little harder. It is harmful only when a person can no longer separate fantasy from reality. When this happens, a person may spend so much psychic energy on fantasy that they don't get on with changing things that are blocking their progress in real life.

RATIONALIZATION

Here, a person finds an excuse for their behaviour that is more acceptable to the ego than the real reason. For example, the driver of a car might say: 'I took the wrong turning there because I was so busy trying to avoid that wretched cyclist who was all over the road.' This conveniently covers up the fact that actually they were not paying attention to where they were going in the first place. Rationalization allows people to avoid responsibility and guilt.

REGRESSION

Regression is another defence mechanism. Here, the person reverts back to an earlier behaviour or developmental stage that feels safe or comforting. We all tend to do it if we feel ill or upset. It is very common in children who want more attention, perhaps because of a new baby, or because their parents are getting divorced. Adults sometimes go into a severe regression after a ghastly trauma and may even curl up into a foetal position.

REACTION FORMATION

Sometimes a person feels an impulse and covers it up by displaying its exact opposite – for example by being pleasant and polite to somebody they actually want to be rude to. Reaction formation as a defence is quite common in teenagers and is often shown by an individual being hostile to somebody they are really attracted to. The problem arises when the latent urge remains dormant and unresolved and so may build up into a powerfully negative force.

TRANSFERENCE

Any of the defence mechanisms can actually be helpful and they all appear in the behaviour of normal, healthy people. Problems only arise when they are overdone and the person becomes blind to their true feelings and motives. The job of the psychoanalyst is to help people to unravel these. This can be a very painful process, but it is one that helps us towards a more balanced personality.

During the course of psychoanalytic treatment, some 'transference' may take place as the client develops emotional attitudes towards the analyst. This is quite normal: in fact, it is often part of the healing process. When this happens, the client may direct feelings of love or hostility towards the analyst. This can be helpful because it recreates the original problem in miniature. Freud called this a 'transference neurosis'. The advantage is that unconscious feelings are now out in the open and can be examined and hopefully dealt with properly.

NARCISSISM

Freud found some patients who did not respond to psychoanalytic therapy at all. He used the myth of Narcissus to explain what was going on. Narcissus was a beautiful youth in ancient Greece who fell in love with his own reflection in a pool. He pined away and eventually died and was turned into a flower because he could never fully possess himself. Freud saw this story as a good way of illustrating the idea of an ego that has become totally self-absorbed and can no longer relate to the outside world. Such cases of psychosis are not treatable by psychoanalysis because the normal transference does not occur.

Narcissism is normal in infancy, when the infantile ego expects the outside world to be just the same as itself. It is also normal for some degree of self-love to appear within any adult relationship.

MOURNING AND MELANCHOLIA

In 1915 Freud wrote *Mourning and Melancholia*, which can be found in *The Standard Edition of the Complete Works of Freud*. We would now call melancholia severe depression. This often occurs after a traumatic life event, such as a bereavement or divorce, and it shows itself in many ways:

● The person blames him- or herself for what has happened and becomes self-destructive, even suicidal.
● He or she becomes very withdrawn from the world, as in narcissism, but this time the self is seen as being bad, unworthy, dirty, etc.
● Severe mourning can conceal repressed hatred for the lost person. The lost person may become identified with the person's own ego, so that hate becomes self-hate and guilt.

This process, where a person absorbs into the self the characteristics of another, is called 'introjection'.

● The person may regress to an infantile state, where biting, sucking and excreting are dominant. They may be absorbed by images of excreta and filth.
● During this melancholic state, a person may not be able to express their mixed feelings of love and hate directly.

INSTINCTS

It is not always clear what Freud means when he talks about 'instincts'. In fact, he says that they are a very vague concept, 'magnificent in their indefiniteness'. He complains that people are forever inventing new instincts in order to explain different aspects of behaviour such as love, hunger, aggression and so on. Freud turned to biology for help, trying as always to be scientific in his approach. This was not easy, because science concerns itself with external, observable reality, whereas Freud was grappling with the workings of the mind.

According to Freud, current biological thinking grouped instincts into two types, according to the aim of the behaviour involved. The first type was aimed at self-preservation, the second at preservation of the species. Freud carried this idea over into psychoanalysis and therefore classified instincts in two ways:

1 **Ego instincts** – concerned with the needs of the individual.
2 **Sexual instincts** – concerned with preserving the species.

Freud tried to clarify what he meant by an instinct by contrasting it with a stimulus. A stimulus, he said, arises from things going on outside the body. Instincts arise from within, so that they cannot be avoided by running away, as is the case with a stimulus.

EROS AND THANATOS

For a long time Freud was puzzled by the tendency for patients to go on repeating and reliving unpleasant experiences. He called this 'repetition compulsion'. He found that it happens

SUNDAY

MONDAY

TUESDAY

WEDNESDAY

THURSDAY

FRIDAY

SATURDAY

after a sudden and unexpected shock. Freud decided that the experience was repeated so that the normal anxiety that prepares us for danger could be built up and dealt with in retrospect. However, the repetition compulsion can sometimes totally take over. This phenomenon eventually led Freud to suggest that another instinct was at work – Thanatos, or the death instinct, taken from the Greek word for 'death'.

The life instinct... and the death instinct

When Thanatos is directed towards the self it produces self-destructive behaviour, such as addictions, in which the person is 'dicing with death'. Turned outwards, it results in aggressive behaviour. The opposite of Thanatos is Eros, the life instinct (from Eros, the Greek god of love). Eros is concerned with survival of the species and is responsible for sexual and reproductive behaviour.

Freud's argument for the existence of Thanatos can be summarized as follows:

● All behaviour is aimed at reducing tension and achieving a previously existing state of stability.
● Since we were all originally made from inert matter, then perhaps we are really trying all the time to return to this state.
● So the aim of all life is death, a state where there are no tensions at all.

This seems like a very negative way of looking at things, but this perhaps arose partly because in the 1920s and 1930s Freud's own life had become very difficult and full of pain.

SUMMARY

Today we have looked at Freud's theories of psychosexual development. We have traced the stages of infantile sexuality and how the successful negotiation of these stages plays a crucial role in the shaping of the adult personality. While many subsequent psychoanalysts and psychologists have reassessed and challenged some of Freud's theories and assumptions, the fundamental notion of a dynamic, active childhood sexuality and its importance in enabling human flourishing continue to be vital and illuminating.

Popular understanding of Freud's ideas has often been reductive –'Everything we do and are is about sex' might well sum it up – but what I hope this chapter has shown is that his thought was much more wide-ranging, nuanced and challenging than this quick-fire summary would suggest. As we have seen, Freud himself was prepared to see his ideas as an ongoing project, an open-ended investigation into the human psyche during which he was open to changing his mind, (occasionally) admitting his ignorance and offering up fresh interpretations.

SUNDAY

MONDAY

TUESDAY

WEDNESDAY

THURSDAY

FRIDAY

SATURDAY

FACT-CHECK (ANSWERS AT THE BACK)

1. Which of the following might indicate oral fixation?
a) Smoking ☐
b) Drinking ☐
c) Overeating ☐
d) All of the above ☐

2. What is the second stage in Freud's account of infantile sexual development?
a) The phallic stage ☐
b) The anal stage ☐
c) The oral stage ☐
d) The genital stage ☐

3. The Oedipus complex occurs at roughly what age?
a) 1–2 years ☐
b) 3–5 years ☐
c) 4–7 years ☐
d) Puberty ☐

4. Oedipus was the son of...
a) Shepherds ☐
b) Polybus and Merope ☐
c) Laius and Jocasta ☐
d) Cadmus and Harmonia ☐

5. How might we best summarize the story of Oedipus?
a) He hated his father and killed him ☐
b) He fell in love with his mother ☐
c) He unknowingly killed his parents and blinded himself when he found out ☐
d) He unknowingly killed his father and married his mother ☐

6. According to Freud, the Oedipus complex occurs...
a) Only in some boys ☐
b) In all young children ☐
c) In all boys ☐
d) None of the above ☐

7. Which of the following does *not* usually apply to Freud's conception of the genital phase?
a) Renewal of sexual interest ☐
b) Resolution of the Oedipus complex ☐
c) A period of anxiety and confusion ☐
d) Attainment of a normal, socialized sexuality ☐

8. Which of the following is the best definition of the id?
a) The self-censoring part of the psyche ☐
b) The ordinary, everyday conscious self ☐
c) The primitive, unconscious part of the psyche ☐
d) The disruptive, selfish part of the personality ☐

9. Which of the following are jobs of the superego?
a) It reprimands the ego ☐
b) It acts as the conscience ☐
c) It monitors the ego ☐
d) It represents the 'voice' of tradition and society ☐

10. Which of the following might be an example of displacement?

a) Accusing someone of being a liar when you have just told a lie ❏

b) Dreaming about a foreign holiday ❏

c) Curling up in a foetal position ❏

d) Kicking an inanimate object in anger ❏

SUNDAY

MONDAY

TUESDAY

WEDNESDAY

THURSDAY

FRIDAY

SATURDAY

FRIDAY

Freud and society

Today we will look at how Freud used the prism of psychoanalysis to develop insights into the tensions between the individual and society as well as into the development of civilization as a whole. Freud said that civilization is necessary for the survival of the species, but it demands sacrifices from the individual because instinctual urges have to be suppressed in order for the person to conform to the rules. Living in society is therefore difficult and it is hard for people to be happy.

Living through World War I, Freud became disillusioned as he observed the gulf between what passed as acceptable behaviour for the state and for the individual. The state also demanded obedience, yet treated people like children by censoring the truth. Freud maintained that, deep down, human nature consists of instinctual impulses and therefore we cannot eradicate evil.

Freud saw art as the result of the sublimation of libidinous urges and likened the artist to a child at play, living in an escapist world. He was also dismissive of religious teachings, saying that they were merely created to help people cope with the tensions inherent in civilization.

CIVILIZATION

Freud saw civilization as representing the ways in which human life has raised itself above its animal origins. Civilization demands great sacrifices from the individual because he or she has to suppress their instinctual urges all the time in order to be able to conform. The purpose of human life is the pursuit of happiness, dominated by the pleasure principle. By happiness, Freud means the satisfaction of libidinous needs that often become dammed up. The ego has to find ways of controlling such urges, sublimating them so that society will approve of behaviour. Living in society is therefore difficult and it is hard for people to be happy.

The features of civilized living are seen by Freud as beauty, order and cleanliness. Justice is the first requirement in maintaining these – the law must not be broken in favour of the individual. The two main reasons for living together in societies are:

1 the need to get together in order to share the workload
2 security within relationships – for example man and woman, parent and child.

In order to gain these advantages, people must curb their sexual and aggressive urges. Consequently, aggressive urges are turned inwards towards the self, causing a sense of guilt and a need for punishment. This is the essence of the Oedipus complex, whereby the instinctual urge is repressed for fear of action by external authority and gradually the internal sense of authority, the superego, takes over.

The conflicting needs of society versus the individual lead to a constant battle between ego and altruism. The essence of this battle is 'Do I answer my own needs, or do I try to fit in with other people?' Freud suggests that this battle is what causes neuroses and that it is possible that entire civilizations can develop a sort of mass neurosis and a communal superego. An obvious example would be the dictator leading the mass of followers. Freud became increasingly disillusioned with human nature and he felt that people constantly overvalued power, status and wealth. These ideas certainly have a prophetic ring to them in the modern world.

THOUGHTS ABOUT WAR

During World War I, Freud at first supported the Austro-German Alliance for which members of his family fought. However, he was a pacifist at heart and became very disillusioned with war.

In 1915 Freud wrote two short pieces describing his thoughts about war. He expressed his bewilderment as the nations of the civilized world slaughtered one another and destroyed so much that science, technology and art had strived to achieve. Freud recognized the gap between what passes as acceptable behaviour for a state and what is expected of the individual. He also saw that the state demanded complete obedience from its people, and yet treated them like children by its censorship of the truth. His sense of disillusionment increased as he observed:

● the low morality shown in the behaviour of states
● the brutality that emerged in the behaviour of individuals, who used war as an excuse to unleash aggression.

Freud said these two observations proved that deep down human nature consists of instinctual impulses; therefore we can never totally eradicate evil. A person can be 'good' in one set of circumstances and 'bad' in another. People conform and obey because they need love and fear punishment.

Freud is not really trying to say that it is impossible for humans to behave in a civilized fashion. He actually says that people have overestimated their own capabilities – we are not as highly evolved as we had thought we were. If we were less demanding of ourselves, this would lead to less disillusionment and the ability to be more open and honest.

Freud lived to see the start of World War II as well. Adolf Hitler had come to power in Germany in 1933 and there was a public burning of Freud's books in Berlin. Freud saw this as progress, saying that in the Middle Ages they would have burned him too. How wrong he was – fortunately Freud was spared the horror of the Holocaust because he and his immediate family fled to England, but several members of his wider family were victims. One wonders what he would have thought and felt about it. His fellowship with other Jews mattered to him and he had belonged to a Jewish club in Vienna, even though he did not follow the Jewish religion.

Another Jew to flee from Nazism was the theoretical physicist Albert Einstein. In a letter written in 1932, he persuaded Freud to write again about war. Freud replied that war was more a problem for statesmen to worry about, but he tried to arrive at some psychological insights, as follows:

- Usually conflicts of interest among humans are settled by the use of violence.
- Several weak people can combine to overcome one strong one.
- A community is held together by emotional ties.
- Problems arise within a community when suppressed members begin to want more power.
- The instincts of love and hate are both essential – you cannot have one without the other.

Freud therefore concluded that war could be prevented only if a central authority was set up which had the right to settle all conflicts of interest. To this end, he suggested educating a special elite, with independent open minds, who would 'give direction to the dependent masses'. (This sounds curiously similar to what the Nazis had in mind.)

ART AND LITERATURE

Freud's work on the unconscious and the use of free-association techniques has had an enormous effect upon both art and literature. Artists began to experiment a lot more with imagery from dreams, visions and the unconscious. This gave rise to movements such as Surrealism, the most famous example of which is the work of Salvador Dalí. This idea was not actually new – as long ago as the fifteenth century, Hieronymus Bosch became famous for his grotesque and fantastic imagery – but Freud's ideas led to a fresh upsurge of interest in such things.

Biographers began to examine the intimate sexual details and childhood experiences of their subjects, and novelists began to use new techniques such as the 'stream of consciousness'. This method, used for example by Virginia Woolf, gives the reader a detailed account of all that the character is thinking from moment to moment. It has obvious connections with the free-association technique.

Freud believed that all art and literature was the result of the sublimation of libidinous urges. Daydreams and fantasies were ways of evading the tedious grip of the reality principle. Artists and writers actually allowed themselves to live in their fantasy world, so effectively evading the reality principle and using their fantasies in creative ways. This cunningly avoids the worse peril of becoming a sexual pervert or neurotic.

The artist is likened to a child at play, living in an escapist world. According to Freud, 'normal' people ought to outgrow this, and happy people never fantasize because it means that they are expressing unfulfilled desires. Happily, modern psychology has shown that a moderate amount of fantasizing can be positive and perfectly healthy.

Freud seems to have overlooked the fact that plenty of artists and writers are neurotic and no doubt there are just as many perverts among them as there are in the general population! Taking his theory to its logical limit, if everyone's libido were fully satisfied then there would be no art or literature – a depressing thought.

RELIGION

Freud wrote three books about his views on religion: *Totem and Taboo* (1913), *The Future of an Illusion* (1927) and *Moses and Monotheism* (1937). In general he was dismissive of religious teachings because they were not scientific and thought about religion only from a psychological point of view. He suggested that people had created 'the gods' to fulfil the need for parental figures, protecting people and watching over them.

At the heart of his criticism of religion is the fact that its teachings cannot be verified. To Freud, religious ideas are illusions, fulfilments of the oldest, most primal needs. Religious questions lead people to be introspective and not scientific, and this can lead them towards self-deception. Freud does rather grudgingly admit that religious teachings have undoubtedly helped to build and maintain civilization,

For Freud, religion was a projection of the superego, instilling fear of wrongdoing but also a sense of paternal protection.

but argued that they have also discouraged freethinking. He also admits that he too may be chasing an illusion, concluding that, although science itself is not an illusion, we may place too much emphasis upon its teachings.

Freud was an atheist and basically dismissed the whole idea of there being a god. He seems to base all his ideas on patriarchal, monotheistic religions and very much emphasizes the idea of God as a father figure. Because he sees religion as an illusion, he suggests that ideally it should be abandoned. He admits, however, that this would be difficult in practice because religion forms the basis for our rules of law and order, and the human race is not sufficiently advanced yet to cope without it.

According to Freud, the principal tasks of civilization are:

● to defend people against the perils of nature, such as famine, flood and disease

- to control and regulate instincts such as incest, cannibalism and lust for killing
- to demonstrate achievements that are considered worth striving for.

The principal tasks of 'the gods' are:

- to protect people from the perils of nature
- to reconcile people to the cruelty of fate, especially death
- to compensate for the suffering imposed by civilization.

Religious rituals give the individual protection from the unruly libidinal urges arising from within and so enable the person to function within a group. Religion has another advantage – it promises an afterlife, which not only lessens the fear of death but also suggests that the person will be rewarded eventually for suppressing some of his instinctual urges. Freud does not seem to have understood the ecstatic and mystical states that many people associate with religion, and barely considers them at all. He dismisses such states, comparing them with being in love. Both states, he says, are examples of regression to a very early stage, where the individual has not learned to distinguish himself from his mother, or from the external world.

Although he had a tendency to generalize on the basis of very slim evidence, Freud claimed to be offering scientific explanations for his ideas about religion; this is rather ironic, considering that he was very dismissive of religious teachings because they were not scientific! He was not very interested in philosophy either, saying dismissively that it was mere playing with words. He argued that people should always try to be down to earth in their thinking and view the world objectively – curiously, he seems here to overlook the role of the unconscious in human thinking.

MONDAY

TUESDAY

WEDNESDAY

THURSDAY

FRIDAY

SATURDAY

SUMMARY

Today we have learned about Freud's ideas about how the structure and workings of the human psyche might be reflected in the development of civilization and could be used to explain a wide range of phenomena such as war, art and religion.

Freud lived through one of the most tumultuous and bloody periods in human history – encompassing World War I and the development of totalitarian ideologies such as fascism and communism, and an intensification of anti-Semitism that, shortly after Freud's death, would culminate in the Holocaust. Little wonder, then, that Freud would seek to 'explain' such traumatic events through the prism provided by psychoanalysis. Freud's insights can be both illuminating and bleak – for example, in explaining how people could be led to commit the most terrible atrocities in the name of 'civilization' and 'order'.

Tomorrow we will return to psychoanalysis itself, tracing how it developed as both theory and therapeutic practice in the hands of Freud's colleagues and successors.

MONDAY

TUESDAY

WEDNESDAY

THURSDAY

FRIDAY

SATURDAY

FACT-CHECK (ANSWERS AT THE BACK)

1. It is hard for people to be happy, Freud thought, because...
a) They are simply not hard-wired to be happy ❏
b) Civilization demands the suppression of their instinctual urges ❏
c) They easily come into conflict with one other ❏
d) They are not civilized enough ❏

2. Freud considered movements such as Nazism to be caused by...
a) An eruption of the id ❏
b) The collapse of civilized values ❏
c) A kind of mass neurosis ❏
d) None of the above ❏

3. How might we best describe the development of Freud's ideas about society?
a) He became more optimistic ❏
b) He came to see that the answer to war lay in religion ❏
c) He believed that societies needed to become more authoritarian ❏
d) He became more pessimistic ❏

4. The fascist dictator Adolf Hitler...
a) Supported Freud's ideas ❏
b) Tried to stamp out Freud's ideas ❏
c) Disliked Freud's ideas because he was Jewish ❏
d) None of the above ❏

5. Freud believed that all art was the result of...
a) Sublimation ❏
b) Self-expression ❏
c) Regression ❏
d) Introspection ❏

6. Which artistic movement was influenced by psychoanalysis?
a) Expressionism ❏
b) Impressionism ❏
c) Futurism ❏
d) Surrealism ❏

7. The 'stream of consciousness' technique used by writers has similarities with the psychoanalytic technique of...
a) Dream analysis ❏
b) Free association ❏
c) Word play ❏
d) None of the above ❏

8. Freud was...
a) Agnostic ❏
b) A religious Jew ❏
c) Atheist ❏
d) None of the above ❏

9. Which of the following is *not* one of Freud's books about religion?
a) *The Golden Bough* ❏
b) *Totem and Taboo* ❏
c) *Moses and Monotheism* ❏
d) *The Future of an Illusion* ❏

10. Which of the following describes Freud's understanding of religion?
a) Regression ❏
b) Consolation ❏
c) Illusion ❏
d) All of the above ❏

SATURDAY

The development of psychoanalysis

While Freud's ideas initially met with widespread hostility, he nonetheless soon attracted a group of followers, who, from 1902, met regularly at his home. In 1908 this group, originally called the Wednesday Society, was renamed the Vienna Psychoanalytical Society. Its first president was Alfred Adler.

By 1909 Freud was well known internationally and the first *International Journal of Psychoanalysis* was published. The following year the International Psychoanalytic Association was formed. Right from the start, there tended to be arguments and rifts within the psychoanalytic movement. However, many influential psychologists and psychiatrists have been inspired by Freud and have developed his ideas further.

Methods that have their roots in Freud's basic techniques are still used by many therapists today. He was a prolific writer and his style is easy to follow. His original case histories, such as those of the 'Rat Man' and the 'Wolf Man', make particularly interesting reading.

EARLY BEGINNINGS OF THE PSYCHOANALYTIC MOVEMENT

In 1902 Freud was appointed as a professor at the University of Vienna. This was mainly because of his work in the field of neurology. People in the medical and academic world were still reacting with hostility and suspicion to his controversial ideas about psychoanalysis. Freud carried on with these ideas more or less alone, but gradually a small band of followers began to gather around him. He began a little group of like-minded people called the Wednesday Psychological Society, and they would meet in his waiting room. Each week one of the members would give a talk about new ideas, followed by refreshments and then a discussion.

The group soon expanded by word of mouth and by 1906 there were 17 members. Eventually, the group evolved into the Vienna Psychoanalytical Society. Otto Rank was appointed secretary and he kept minutes of the meetings and accounts. By 1907 the group was getting more cosmopolitan – a Russian named Max Eitingon joined them, followed by some Swiss recruits from the Burghölzli Mental Hospital in Zurich. These were Ludwig Binswanger, Carl Jung and Karl Abraham. Freud and Jung got on especially well and a kind of father–son relationship developed between them, Freud being nearly 20 years older than Jung. Freud was particularly pleased that Jung was a Gentile because this rescued the psychoanalytic movement from accusations that it was an all-Jewish organization.

Over the next year, the Hungarian doctor Sándor Ferenczi joined the group, and then Ernest Jones, a young Welsh neurologist, and Abraham Brill from the United States. Eitingon and Abraham went on to establish psychoanalysis in Berlin and Ferenczi in Budapest. Jones and Brill were the first to introduce psychoanalytic thinking into the English language. The first International Congress of Freudian Psychology took place in Salzburg in 1908.

By 1909 Freud was well known internationally and he went with Jung and Ferenczi to America to lecture. The first issue of the *International Journal of Psychoanalysis* was published the same year, and Freud was awarded an honorary degree from Clark University, Massachusetts. The next year the International Psychoanalytic Association was formed. International progress was fairly slow until the end of World War I. In 1920 the Institute of Psychoanalysis was opened in Berlin, followed by ones in London, Vienna and Budapest. Courses were held for students and free treatment offered for people who could not afford the fees. Institutes were opened in the United States in New York (1931) and Chicago (1932).

RIFTS IN THE PSYCHOANALYTIC MOVEMENT

Right from the start, there tended to be arguments and disagreements within the psychoanalytic movement. People were keen to develop their own theories and some accused others of inventing case histories to fit their theories. Arguments arose about the way the society should be organized, and about psychoanalytic methods and concepts such as the unconscious. To make matters worse, the group was constantly under outside attack, from the scientific establishment and the press.

OTTO RANK

Otto Rank (1884–1939) had been a protégé of Freud, who had encouraged and supported his education. For a long time he was loyal to Freud, but eventually he was thrown out of the group. His main complaint was that he felt the period of analysis was too long and he suggested that it should be shortened. He also saw childhood traumas, especially the Oedipus complex, as being less important than Freud made out. For him, it was the trauma of birth itself that mattered.

CARL JUNG

Carl Jung (1875–1961) was Freud's favourite for some years. Freud treated him like a son and wanted him to be his successor. In 1910 he was appointed as the President of the newly formed

International Psychoanalytic Society. However, there had already been suggestions of problems in his relationship with Freud before then.

The year before, while they were waiting to board ship to go to America, tension was in the air. Freud had found out that Jung had been having an illicit affair with one of his patients. Jung retaliated by being hostile towards Freud, irritating him by going on and on about some mummified peat bog men that were being dug up in North Germany. Freud got very het up and eventually fainted. Later, he said that this was because Jung had a death wish against him.

Worse was to come as Jung began to develop new theories of his own. In 1912 he gave a series of lectures and seminars at Fordham University in New York. It was at this point that he really broke away from Freud, criticizing some of his basic theories of psychoanalysis such as the emphasis on sex. Not long after this attack, Freud talked to Jung at length at a conference in Munich and felt that he had won him back into the fold. Freud then proceeded to faint again at lunch, and Jung had to carry him through into another room. Clearly Freud was deeply upset about the whole affair.

The next year, Jung lectured in London and coined the phrase 'analytical psychology' to describe the divergent ideas that he was evolving. After this, letters between Freud and Jung became increasingly bitter. Jung accused Freud of behaving like a controlling father, intolerant towards new ideas. Sadly, in 1913 their friendship ceased altogether and the two men became openly hostile to one another. Before long, Jung resigned his presidency of the International Psychoanalytic Society.

WILHELM REICH

Reich (1897–1957) was another member of the orthodox psychoanalytic movement who broke away, though much later, in 1933. He was interested in the way individuals interacted with society and believed that a person's character was formed in this way. For him, the sexual revolution was connected with the social revolution. He worked with the communist party, thus combining psychoanalysis with politics.

Most of the people who broke away from Freud did so because they felt that he laid too much emphasis on sex. Psychoanalysis was very difficult to understand and people were constantly coming up with new variations of their own. Freud tended to present a rather authoritarian figure, always trying to keep control and resenting the intrusion of new ideas from others. It is amusing to think of him as a sort of struggling superego of the psychoanalytic movement, desperately trying to control all the other egos!

SOME FAMOUS FOLLOWERS OF FREUD

ANNA FREUD

Freud's youngest daughter, Anna (1895–1982), became a psychoanalyst and an important member of the International Psychoanalytic Association. She supported her father's original ideas, but developed and extended them. She concentrated mainly on the ego rather than the id, and believed that it was important to look at defence mechanisms in order to understand what the problems are that the ego is grappling with.

With her ailing father, Anna fled from the Nazis before World War II and eventually co-founded the Hampstead Child Therapy Clinic. Her ideas are important mainly because she derived them from direct observation of young children, rather than by talking to adults about their childhood. She was a pioneer in working with psychologically disturbed children.

MELANIE KLEIN

Melanie Klein (1882–1960) was born in Vienna but she moved to London in 1926 and became a British citizen. Like Anna Freud, her main contribution came from her work with children – she believed that emotions were present in children from a very young age. She observed children's emotions by watching them at play, even before they could express themselves verbally. This new method led to her being able to analyse children at a much earlier age than had previously been thought possible, even as young as two years old.

Melanie Klein believed that the forerunner of the superego began to form during the first two years of life. For her the aggressive drive was the important one, rather than the sexual drive. She was one of the leading lights in the Object Relations School, which disagreed with Freud's stages of child development. It said that right from birth the mental life of a child is oriented towards an 'object', which can be anything in the external world – a person or a thing. The child constructs its inner world from ideas about these external objects. Conflicts arise as a result of the way in which this 'internalization' process progresses.

KAREN HORNEY

Karen Horney (1885–1952) was an analyst in Berlin during the 1920s and 1930s and she later joined the staff at the New York Psychoanalytical Institute. She was particularly interested in social factors in psychological development and eventually her ideas evolved away from the mainstream. Many people in the psychoanalytical movement have taken a rather 'closed shop' attitude, saying that people who are not analysts will never be able fully to understand psychoanalytical theory. Karen Horney, however, wrote for the general reader and her ideas became very popular in America.

Karen Horney maintained that social influences are much more important than underlying fixed biological patterns in developing neuroses. She said that the latter idea was too deterministic and out of date. She argued against the idea of an Oedipus complex, saying that there was no such thing as a universal child psychology. She was also interested in women's psychology. She said that women's feelings of inferiority were caused by social oppression, rather than by a biologically determined castration complex.

ERICH FROMM

Erich Fromm (1900–80) was born in Germany and trained as a social psychologist and psychoanalyst. Fromm was interested in the individual's relationship with society. He said that different cultures produce different psychological types, and the work of anthropologists since has tended to back up his ideas. The Oedipus complex has indeed turned out not to be universal – there are big differences in child-rearing habits, family structure, social rules and so on.

Fromm's ideas differed from those of Freud in two fundamental ways:

1 A person's main challenge comes from the way he or she relates to others in society and not from the struggle with instinctual urges.
2 Relationships between mankind and society are constantly changing. Freud had taken the view that the relationship was static – mankind was basically evil and society's job was to tame the individual.

PSYCHOANALYSIS TODAY

Modern psychoanalysts do not usually completely adhere to Freud's recommendations about how to conduct therapy sessions. Nevertheless, many basic techniques used today by analysts and other psychotherapists – including the free-association technique, transference and the analysis of dreams – are still similar to those used by Freud.

Freud always tried to maintain the scientific approach and remain as detached as possible. Many modern analysts adopt a more relaxed attitude and, unlike Freud, sit facing their patients. However, most analysts still try to guard against becoming too emotionally involved, or revealing much of their own personal life to the patient, because this can easily take the analysis off track.

Many people have criticized Freud, saying, among other things, that:

● he places far too much emphasis upon sex
● he claims to be scientific and yet his findings are often vague, inaccurate and based upon small samples of data
● many of his ideas were not actually original
● psychoanalysis doesn't work – in fact, it may even make symptoms worse
● the movement has tended to have a very 'closed shop' attitude – you cannot grasp the theories properly unless you are an analyst yourself.

Despite such criticisms, Freud's ideas have taken root: so much so that the very language of psychoanalysis has become subtly absorbed into ordinary speech. We all use phrases such as 'Freudian slip', 'death wish' and 'anally retentive', and many modern therapies have their roots in psychoanalytic thinking. Without Freud, perhaps we would not yet have begun to understand such things as:

- the importance of childhood experiences in the development of the adult personality
- the existence of the unconscious and its huge influence over human behaviour
- the way we all use endless defence mechanisms to protect our egos
- the importance of dreams in understanding our true thoughts and feelings
- the fact that talking about a problem often leads to helping to sort it out.

Whatever people may say, psychoanalysis is more popular than ever, especially in the United States. There are numerous books about it and the ideas are now much more accessible to the general public and open to debate. It seems that psychoanalysis, in one form or another, is here to stay.

SUMMARY

SUNDAY

MONDAY

TUESDAY

WEDNESDAY

THURSDAY

FRIDAY

SATURDAY

As we have seen today, Freud himself constantly developed and reassessed his ideas, so it is little wonder that others, too, should take his ideas in new directions or bring different emphases to his thought. Freud could be dogmatic and authoritarian, however, and some of his followers –most notably Jung – came to feel that they would have to rebel against the 'father' of psychoanalysis if they were to be free to develop their own ideas. Others took psychoanalysis into areas where Freud had shown himself weaker (sometimes by his own admission), such as the fields of female sexuality or the psychoanalysis of children.

Throughout this week we have explored the broad outlines of Freud's ideas – from his early elaboration of psychoanalytic techniques, through his theories about psychosexual development, including the Oedipus complex, to his later investigations into the psychological roots of civilization. In their richness, courageousness and determination to plumb the depths of human motivation, his ideas continue to have the power to inspire, challenge and provoke.

FACT-CHECK (ANSWERS AT THE BACK)

1. In what year was the first issue of the *International Journal of Psychoanalysis* published?
   a) 1908 ❑
   b) 1909 ❑
   c) 1910 ❑
   d) 1911 ❑

2. Which psychoanalyst emphasized the importance of the trauma of birth?
   a) Ernst Jones ❑
   b) Otto Rank ❑
   c) Carl Jung ❑
   d) Karl Abraham ❑

3. With which psychoanalyst did Freud develop an almost father–son-type relationship?
   a) Ernst Jones ❑
   b) Otto Rank ❑
   c) Carl Jung ❑
   d) Karl Abraham ❑

4. Carl Jung disagreed with Freud primarily about...
   a) The right to have illicit affairs with patients ❑
   b) The existence of the collective unconscious ❑
   c) The centrality of the sex drive ❑
   d) None of the above ❑

5. Which of the following best describes the achievement of Anna Freud?
   a) She took psychoanalysis in a whole new direction ❑
   b) She rigidly applied her father's ideas to the psychoanalysis of children ❑
   c) She pioneered working with psychologically disturbed children ❑
   d) None of the above ❑

6. Which of the following does *not* apply to the work of Melanie Klein?
   a) She worked from close observation of children at play ❑
   b) She emphasized the role of the sex drive ❑
   c) She analysed children as young as two ❑
   d) She was an important figure in the Object Relations School ❑

7. Ernst Fromm emphasized...
   a) The Oedipus complex ❑
   b) The relationship between the individual and his or her society ❑
   c) The role of the id ❑
   d) The importance of culture in determining psychological type ❑

8. Which of the following best describes the achievement of William Reich?
a) He never broke with Freud ❑
b) He was an ardent communist ❑
c) He explored the connections between psychoanalysis and politics ❑
d) He was president of the International Psychoanalytic Society ❑

9. Which of the following best describes the achievement of Karen Horney?
a) She gave psychoanalysis a proper technical language ❑
b) She helped make psychoanalytic ideas accessible to ordinary people ❑
c) She challenged Freud's ideas about female psychology ❑
d) She founded the New York Psychoanalytic Institute ❑

10. For which of the following has Freud *not* been criticized?
a) He gave too much importance to sex and sexuality ❑
b) His ideas are 'unscientific' ❑
c) Psychoanalysis can be positively harmful ❑
d) His courage and originality in pioneering new theories about childhood psychology ❑

SUNDAY

MONDAY

TUESDAY

WEDNESDAY

THURSDAY

FRIDAY

SATURDAY

GLOSSARY

complex Group of related emotional ideas or impulses that are usually repressed but which continue to influence an individual's behaviour

condensation The fusion of two or more ideas in a dream

Conscious mind The part of the mind that is aware of its actions and emotions

defence mechanism An unconscious way of protecting the ego against undesirable affects

denial A **defence mechanism** in which the individual refuses to recognize a feeling or situation

displacement A **defence mechanism** in which the emotions attached to one idea are shifted on to a different idea

ego The conscious part of the psyche, responsible for regulating the instinctual desires of the **id** and in turn regulated by the **superego**

Eros The life instinct; *compare* **Thanatos**

fixation Where an individual becomes stuck in a psychosexual developmental phase

free association A psychoanalytic technique where the client is given a word and then tells the analyst all the ideas that come to mind, thereby uncovering a route into the unconscious

id The unconscious part of the psyche made up of the instinctual drives, desires and energies

inversion Freudian term for homosexuality

latency period The period of development when sexual activity is dormant

latent content The part of a dream that is not consciously remembered before analysis

libido The sex drive

manifest content The part of a dream that is consciously remembered

neurosis A usually mild nervous or mental disorder

Oedipus complex The desire of the child to possess sexually the parent of the opposite sex, while excluding the parent of the same sex

parapraxis An accident or error caused by a repressed impulse; commonly known as a 'Freudian slip'

preconscious The part of the unconscious that is most easily accessible to the conscious mind

projection A **defence mechanism** in which the individual attributes an unpleasant feeling or personality trait to another person when, in fact, it is their own

psychosis Severe mental disorder

regression A **defence mechanism** in which the individual reverts to an earlier developmental stage in order to feel safe and secure

repression A **defence mechanism** in which an unpleasant event or emotion is stored away in the unconscious, so that it is inaccessible to the conscious

resistance A psychic process that prevents unconscious ideas from being released

sublimation The unconscious rechanneling of an impulse

transference The redirection of emotions to a substitute, often towards the analyst during psychotherapy

superego The part of the superego that regulates the **ego**, acting as a conscience

Thanatos The death instinct; *compare* **Eros**

ANSWERS

Sunday: 1d; 2c; 3c & d; 4b; 5c; 6d; 7a & d; 8c; 9c; 10d

Monday: 1b; 2a, c & d; 3b; 4c; 5b; 6b, c & d; 7d; 8a; 9d; 10b & c

Tuesday: 1b; 2d; 3d; 4b; 5b, c & d; 6c; 7b; 8c; 9d; 10b

Wednesday: 1b; 2d; 3a; 4c; 5c & d; 6a & b; 7c; 8c; 9a; 10 A case might be made for a, b, c or d!

Thursday: 1d; 2b; 3b; 4c; 5d; 6b; 7c; 8c; 9a, b, c & d; 10a & d

Friday: 1b; 2c; 3d; 4b & c; 5a; 6d; 7b; 8c; 9a; 10d

Saturday: 1b; 2b; 3c; 4c; 5c; 6b; 7b & d; 8c; 9b; 10d